AGE CHANGES IN SOFT TISSUE PROFILE

SOFT TISSUE CHANGES IN ORTHODONTICS

DR. V. SANTHOSH KUMAR

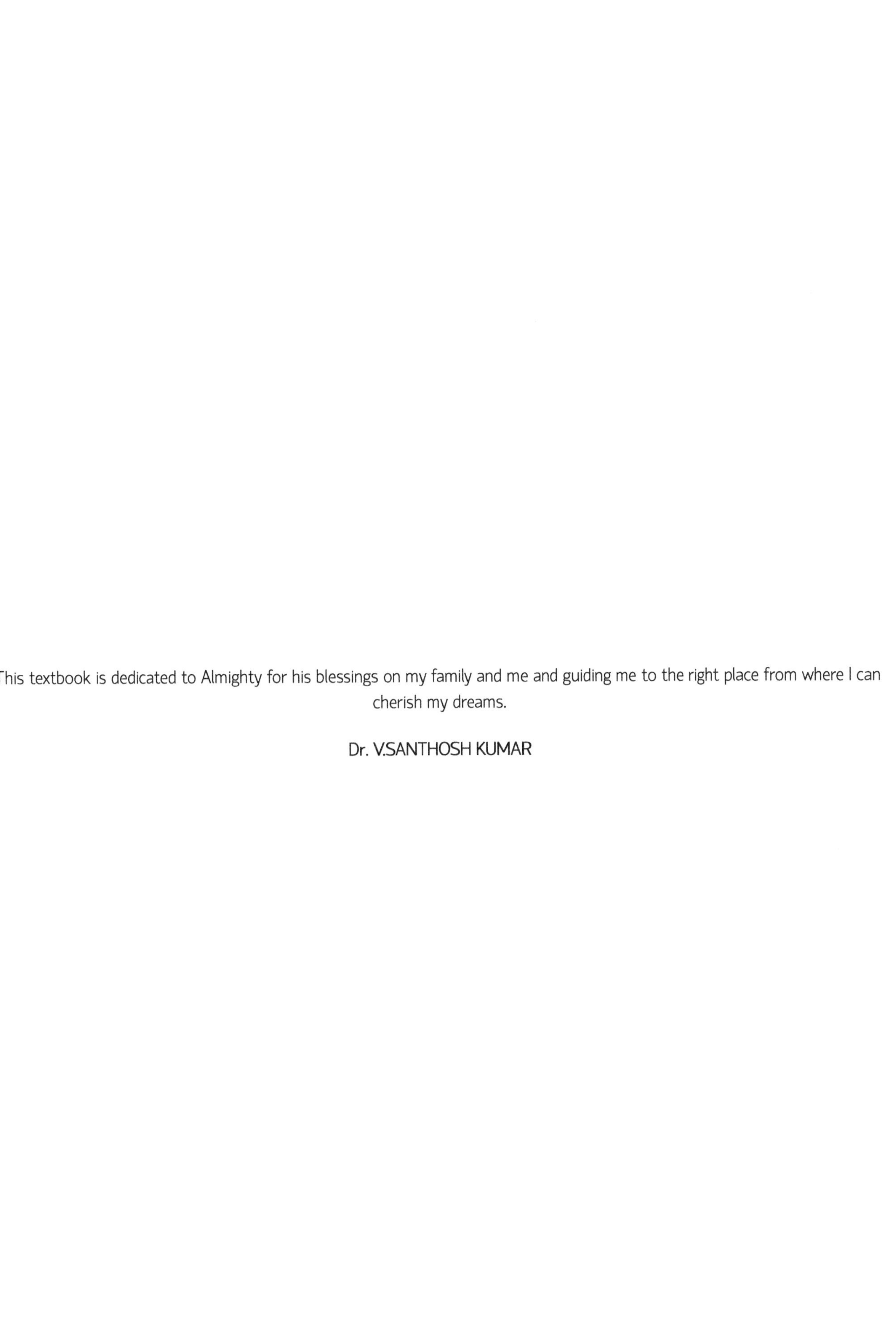

This textbook is dedicated to Almighty for his blessings on my family and me and guiding me to the right place from where I can cherish my dreams.

Dr. V.SANTHOSH KUMAR

Contents

Preface

This textbook is written as a part of my Post Graduate curriculum and it will be a valiant tool in exploring soft tissue parameters before and after orthodontic treatment. The chapters in this textbook will make you to understand the basis of soft tissues around the craniomaxillofacial region and its importance in orthodontic treatment

Acknowledgements

I express my sincere thanks to our esteemed Principal **Dr. ANIL MELATH**, Mahe Institute of Dental Sciences and Hospital, for his encouragement and support.

I consider it as my privilege and honour to express infinite gratitude to my post graduate Guide and mentor **Dr. PANJAMI MARISH. MDS**, Reader, Department of Orthodontics and Dentofacial Orthopedics, Mahe Institute of Dental Sciences, Mahe for her unlimited help and support, sound advice, constant encouragement and valuable guidance right from the beginning till the completion of this library dissertation which can never be sufficiently acknowledged.

With great pleasure I acknowledge **Dr. JITESH KUMAR.K. MDS**, Professor & Head, Department of Orthodontics and Dentofacial Orthopedics, Mahe Institute of Dental Sciences, Mahe for his expertise and advice throughout the period of my post graduation.

I acknowledge, with due respect, the contributions made by my post-graduate teachers,Dr. SURESH BABU C. MDS, Dr. RAMIA RAJENDARAN. MDS, Dr. MOOSAAHMAD. MDS, Dr. NAVYA P. MDS, Department of Orthodontics and Dentofacial Orthopedics, Mahe Institute of Dental Sciences, Mahe by way of their constant help, co- operation, valuable and able guidance, personal attention and supervision throughout the course of this text book. It is my privilege to have worked under their able guidance and supervision.

I wish to thank my seniors **Dr. ARAVINTHAN, Dr. RIZWANA, Dr. SWATHI, Dr. ASWIN, Dr. SITHRA, Dr. DIVYA** and my batch mates **Dr. JEFFERY SAMUEL, Dr. JENISH HARRY** for their help, co-operation and encouragement.

Nothing in life could be credited solely to me; I owe it all to my family and friends. This acknowledgement would not be complete without mentioning my parents **Mr. Vengadesan** and **Mrs. Catherine** and my brother **Siva.** Nothing is permanent other than the constant love and support shown by my people; I thank **Dr.Kirthiga.M** for her valuable support and guidance. I thank **Dr.A.Thangavelu, Dr.Sureshkumar, Dr.Priya darshini, Dr.K.G.Sriraam, Dr.L.Jawahar raman, Dr.M.Narendran,** for their valuable presence in my journey. With a humble heart I bow before them as it is their love, sacrifice and prayers that made my education possible.

CONTENTS

SL.No.	TOPIC
1	INTRODUCTION
2	ESTHETICS
3	HISTORICAL BACKGROUND
4	CHILD FACE
5	THE AGING FACE
6	MALE VS FEMALE
7	FACIAL TYPES
8	PROFILE CHANGES IN GROWING FACE
9	GROWTH CHANGES IN SOFT TISSUE PROFILE
10	ORTHODONTIC RELEVANCE
11	CURRENT CONCEPTS
12	CONCLUSION
13	BIBLIOGRAPHY

Enter Caption

• 3 •

CHAPTER TWO

INTRODUCTION

Age-related changes of jaws and soft tissue profile are important both for orthodontists and general dentists. Behrents reported that craniofacial growth does not stop in young adulthood but is a continuous process even into later ages. The units of change are small but change in the craniofacial skeleton has become the operational concept rather than termination of the process. The increasing demand for adult orthodontics and orthognathic surgery increases the need to understand the facial aging process[1] An understanding of craniofacial growth and development is essential in orthodontics to attain treatment objectives. Craniofacial growth of the skeleton and soft tissue influences the final configuration of occlusion and overall facial aesthetics. The interrelationship of soft tissue components of the face, such as nose, lip, and chin, changes during growth as well as with orthodontic treatment. Thus, it becomes imperative for orthodontists to understand normal growth trends of the nose, lip, and chin.

Past studies have indicated that although major growth and development of the face is due to an increase in size of underlying skeletal structures, soft tissue growth does play a major role in overall facial aesthetics. Although orthodontic literature is replete with longitudinal studies of skeletal growth and development of the face, only a small number of studies have described the facial soft tissue growth.[2]

Harmonious facial aesthetics and optimal functional occlusion have long been recognized as the two most important goals of orthodontic treatment. To accomplish some of these goals, a knowledge of the normal craniofacial growth as well as the effects of orthodontic treatment on the soft tissue profile is essential. Facial features have been commonly studied in full face and profile views. A number of methods have been used to evaluate these facial changes including anthropometry, photogrammetry, computer imaging, and cephalometry. Profiles have been evaluated by using both cephalometric or photometric linear and angular measurements, and combinations of metric, angular, and proportional measurements. In addition, the profile was also qualitatively evaluated by using silhouettes, probably the most simplified method for assessing facial aesthetics because it specifically focuses on the overall outline of the profile.

Angle was one of the first to write about facial harmony and the importance of the soft tissue integument. He used the terms balance, harmony, beauty, and ugliness to note that "The study of orthodontia is indissolubly connected with that of art as related to the human face. The mouth is a most potent factor in making or marring the beauty and character of the face."

In 1944, Tweed gave special attention to aesthetics. He stated that "a thorough concept of the normal growth pattern of the child's face or any face is as important to orthodontists, if not more so, as complete mastery of the science of occlusion." It is important to note that up to that point in time, most of the studies dealt with skeletal analysis. It was assumed, that the soft tissue profile configuration was primarily related to the underlying skeletal configuration.

In 1959, Subtelny indicated that the correlation between hard and soft tissue changes is not strictly a linear one. He measured horizontal and vertical facial relationships and found that not all parts of the soft tissue profile directly follow the underlying skeletal structures. Burstone also observed that a close relationship of the soft tissue profile to the underlying skeletal pattern might not exist because of the variation in the thickness of the soft tissue covering the skeletal face.[3]

There is an increased demand for orthodontic treatment nowadays. Apart from the fact that orthodontics deals with functional and aesthetic problems, most patients, if not all, are seeking orthodontic treatment for aesthetic reasons. This might be attributed to the lack of awareness on orthodontics among these patients, and/or lack of orthodontist's role to enhance such awareness among the community. Instead, many orthodontists, consciously or unconsciously, pay their attention to the aesthetic desire of their patients, sometimes on account of the functional occlusion.

Facial profile is an important factor in orthodontic diagnosis and treatment planning as it is determined by the base of the upper lip and the chin position, extreme forward or backward position of these points makes profile unattractive for both patients and orthodontists. There are other soft tissue factors that should be considered when planning orthodontics; these includes: nasal prominence, nasolabial angle, upper and lower lip position, labio-mental sulcus depth and gum display at rest and on smiling,.etc.[4]

CHAPTER THREE

ESTHETICS

Face has been defined as a chart of destiny, an impression of fullness of life, and mirror of soul. The loss of teeth, because of the effect on facial appearance often causes psychological trauma. Nature has endowed everyone with dignity and satisfaction of being an individual personality. Beauty lies in the eyes of the beholder.

The term "esthetics" was coined in 1750 to designate the science of sensuous knowledge, which gave beauty, in contrast to the science of logic, which gave truth. It is derived from the Greek word "Aesthesis", According to the Glossary Of Prosthodontic Terms, esthetics can be defined as pertaining to the study of beautiful. Descriptive of a specific creation that results from such a study objectifies beauty and attractiveness and elicits pleasure. Websters Third New International Dictionary defines esthetics as appreciative of, responsive to or zealous about the beautiful; having a sense of beauty or fine culture. Esthetic fundamentals are beauty, naturalness and individuality and it is idealizing or harmonizing of the artificial with the natural. Esthetic is the science with established rules and an art necessitating skill and taste in accordance with esthetic principles.[5]

HISTORY

Ancient Civilizations Prehistoric man rarely delineated the features of the human representations he carved in stone or painted on rock. Artworks finally became refined enough to depict likeness or resemblance in the ancient civilizations of Egypt, China, and Greece. However, portraiture in antiquity was often stylized and idealized to try to improve on the common reality. Although kings and deities were portrayed with some of the ideal features of the times, portraits of lesser people were more realistically rendered. A brief selective history of facial portraiture in Western civilization can illustrate esthetic tastes and realities and the shadows in between.

Egyptians

Egyptian artists, beginning in the Old Kingdora dynasties (2600 to 2000 Bc), used a simplified grid system to draw figures to ideal proportions, several horizontal lines marked the location of key points of the body from the top of the head to the baseline. Lines representing the crown of the head, the hairline, and the junction of the neck and shoulders guided the proportional construction of the head. One vertical axial line, registered on the ear position, divided the traditionally profiled figure into two parts. By the time of the Middle and New Kingdoms, a squared grid composed of regularly spaced horizontal and vertical lines was in use (Fig 1).

An additional facial horizontal now appeared near the base of the nose, and many verticals were added. The head usually was depicted within a grid block consisting of 12 squares. This squared grid system, perhaps the oldest forerunner of the proportional mesh diagram designed by Moorrees for cephalometric analysis, guided the ancient Egyptians in applying their canon of ideal proportions to the pictorial representation of the human figure. The Egyptian proportional canon was modified only slightly over the 3,000 years of Egyptian civilization. Facial proportions were generally the same for representations of men and women throughout this period.

Drawing of ancient Egyptian from a tomb ceiling dating from the New Kingdom (1500 Be) and constructed using a proportional grid system developed by the artists of the time. The head and face were carefully composed on the squared grid to meet canonical guidelines set down by the Egyptians for ideal proportions. Artists drew and painted faces usually as part of complete figures, so facial features were precisely proportioned yet lacking details, except on larger works such as statuary. Their use of squared grids and exact proportions helped the Egyptians toward their goal of deifying beauty and harmony.

Greece

Ancient Greece formalized the study of beauty as a learned pursuit and developed intricate formulas for constructing human and godly representations. The Greek philosophers, notably Plato (427-347 Be) and Aristotle (384-322 BC), questioned the intrinsic meaning of beauty and studied the theory of beauty and the philosophy of taste. Interestingly, the Art and Science of Facial Esthetics. Greeks did not apply any particular word, like "esthetics," to describe these intellectual concerns. It was only in the mid-18th century that the term "aesthetica" was coined by German scholar Alexander Baumgarten in a Latin treatise on the beauty of poetry, and soon afterward the concept and the word were applied broadly to the arts and nature.

Two leading Greek sculptors of the 5th century Bc, Polykleitos (450 to 420 Bc) and Phidias (500 to 432 Bc), established strict canons and rues for ideal bodily proportions and harmonious anatomic relationships. The great artists of ancient Greece attempted to implement these laws of beauty in their works. Classical Greek art and architecture blossomed in the fifth

and fourth centuries Bc, a period now labelled the golden age of Greece. The classic Greek face is oval, slightly tapering toward the chin (Fig 2). Like the Egyptians, the basic facial features of men and women appear to be treated the same. In profile, the face exhibits a prominent forehead, a sizable portion of which is concealed by a low hairline. Also characteristic is a relatively straight sweep from the forehead to the nose tip, allowing only a faint concavity at the root of the nose. The lower face is orthognathic in profile, usually displaying some retrusion around the lips. Between the prominent chin and the rolled lower lip is a sharply angled mentolabial sulcus.

The Renaissance

Skipping over the dissipation of Grecian classicism in the Hellenistic period, and the less remarkable artistic achievements of the Romans, who are remembered more as imitators than as creators, the next facial esthetic inspirations may be found in the Italian High Renaissance of the 15th century. Leonardo da Vinci (1452 to 1519) typified the new integration of art and science, with his interminable search for mathematical explanations of natural phenomena. He was driven by a powerful curiosity and imagination that left enduring artistic records. Leonardo studied the face from all angles to unlock some arithmetic magical formula for facial form and beauty, a pursuit that was predictably unsuccessful, judging by today's scientific standards. His anatomical sketches document these experiments and conjectures. Many of his realistic ink drawings show geometric studies superimposed on heads and faces, depicting men whose aged faces often suggest the effects of severe tooth wear and muhiple tooth loss (Fig 3).

The Golden Section and Divine Proportions

During the Renaissance, Leonardo da Vinci and his contemporaries vainly searched for mathematical explanations of nature, including the human facial form. One of the methods frequently referenced was the "golden section" or "divine proportion," a precise structural ratio said to exist throughout nature and to have been observed by the ancients. The Greeks,

from the time of Pythagoras, Plato, and Euclid, seem to be the earliest to have identified the golden section within certain geometric shapes and forms that, in their eyes, possessed optimum visual harmony and pleasing proportions. The proportion was based on the number 1.618, or its reciprocal 0.618, the same numbers expressed in an arithmetic progression that has fascinated mathematicians and numerologists since the 13th century.

It was first described in detail by the Italian mathematician Leonardo Fibonacci, hence its name, the Fibonacci series and Fibonacci numbers. Ricketts attempted to introduce this mathematical curiosity as a tautology on which to base facial analysis for orthodontics and surgery. He believed that the esthetic proportional norms for facial structures (eg, the ratio between forehead-to-eye and eye-to-menton distances), as measured from photographs and cephalograms, were remarkably close to the 1: 1.618 divine proportion.

Man's dream for a mathematical key to the design of natural beauty seems then to have produced at least two distinctly different answers from two cultures, each with elaborate dogma to back up its claims. Although Fibonacci numbers still hold fascination tot mathematicians, their application to facial esthetics can hardly be convincing to bioscientists today. At this point in the late 20th century, the glorified concept of the golden section or divine proportion as a perfectly commensurate mathematical relationship expressed across nature, whether set at 1:1.618, 1:1.414, or some other beguiling ratio, displays earmarks of pseudoscience, possessing doubtful value beyond its historical significance.[6]

The esthetic paradigm

The effect of an esthetic smile cannot be overemphasized and may have far-reaching ramifications in the personal and professional arena. An esthetic smile has been described as one in which the size, shape, position, and color of the teeth are in harmony, proportion, and relative symmetry to each other and the elements that frame them. Mesiodistal and vertical tooth proportions constitute a major determinant of dental esthetics and symmetry. Generating esthetic tooth proportions during the restoration or replacement of the maxillary anterior dentition continues to present significant challenges to the restorative dentist, periodontist, and orthodontist. Depending on the situation, alteration of existing tooth dimensions may involve osseous and orthognathic surgery, orthodontic space distribution, intrusion or extrusion, enameloplasty, and prosthodontic rehabilitation including alteration of the occlusal vertical dimension. Several authors have proposed theoretical guidelincs that purport to help establish esthetic proportions during restoration of the dentition.

The golden proportion

The golden proportion (GP) as a concept was first used in ancient Greek architecture. The basic premise is that for two related objects to appear natural and harmonious, the larger to the smaller should form a ratio of 1.6 and 181:1. In dentistry, GP represents a 62% regression from the mesial to the distal, with the implication that a 62% progressive reduction in the perceived mesiodistal widths of the maxillary anterior teeth is considered to be esthetically pleasing.

As stated by Levin, when viewed from the facial,"The width of the central incisor should be in GP to the width of the lateral incisor, and the width of the lateral incisor should be golden to the canine and the canine width should be golden to the first premolar" (Figure 4). Lombardi proposed that dental and facial esthetics were optimized if features, such as the central to lateral width and lateral to canine width, were repeated in proportion when the patient is viewed from the front.

FIG-4 Graphic representation of the golden proportion

The recurring esthetic dental proportion (RED)

The recurring esthetic dental (RED) proportion was a concept proposed by Ward. The RED proportion states that the proportion of the successive widths of the maxillary teeth as viewed from the front should remain constant progressing distally (Figure 5).When viewed from the front, the width of each successive tooth depreciates by the same proportion relative to the tooth mesial to it. Although the actual proportion may differ (e.g., 70%, 75%, 80%, etc.) because of differences in tooth height and other factors, the selected RED proportion must be applied consistently to the specific smile.

FIG-5 Graphic representation of the recurring esthetic dental (RED) proportion

Width-to-height (w : h) ratio

The W : H ratio of individual teeth, specifically the maxillary central incisors, is a very important intra tooth proportion with significant influence on the balance and esthetics of a smile. (figure 6)

FIG-6 Schematic illustration of the width and height measurements

Vertical position of the maxillary lateral incisor

In an esthetic smile, it has been suggested that the maxillary central incisors and canines be positioned approximately in level with each other, with the incisal edge of the lateral incisors positioned approximately 1 to

1.5 mm superior (Figure 7). This lateral incisor offset is often reflected in orthodontic bracket placement guides. However, the esthetic impact of variations in the vertical position of the maxillary lateral incisor remains unclear.

FIG-7 Minimal lateral incisor vertical offset. B, One mm lateral incisor offset.

The apparent contact dimension

Although there are multiple paradigms that purport to represent optimal maxillary anterior mesiodistal inter tooth proportions, the research on ideal vertical inter tooth proportions is very scant. One such paradigm, the apparent contact dimension or the ACD, is an important indicator of maxillary anterior vertical tooth proportions. ACD, previously referred to as the "connector zone," is defined as the area where the teeth appear to touch when viewed from the facial aspect at 90 degrees to each interproximal area. In an esthetic smile, the ACD between the maxillary anterior has been purported to exhibit a proportional relationship relative to the height of the central incisors. (Figure 8).

This relationship referred to as the 50:40:30 rule defines the ideal ACD between the central incisors as 50% of the height of the central incisors, the ideal ACD between a maxillary lateral incisor and central incisor as 40% of the height of a central incisor, and the ideal ACD between a lateral incisor and a canine as 30% of the height of a central incisor. Proportions of the ACD between the maxillary anterior teeth has a significant influence on tooth shape and the perception of tooth height.[7]

FIG-8 The apparent contact dimension

CHAPTER FOUR

HISTORICAL BACKGROUND

The earliest findings of human beautification were found from Neanderthals some 40,000 years ago in Murcia, Spain, where sea shells were found, containing brightly colored pigments believed to have served as makeup to augment or even camouflage facial structures.

Marcus Vitruvius Pollio, better known as Vitruv, was a Roman architect and engineer from 100 BCE. Not only did he build war machines for Gaius Julius Caesar, but also important water channels and fountains under Emperor Augustus for Rome from 33 BCE on. His theoretical works include a first version of man's typical and balanced proportions; hence, the model is to date named the "Vitruvian man."

He postulated that the center of balance and gravity for men is the umbilicus. The first renowned artist and scientist alike to really establish mathematical rules defining a perfect body and face was Leonardo da Vinci. He further developed the model of the Vitruvian man.

Fig. 1 Leonardo's Vitruvian Man,

Leonardo da Vinci (1452–1519) divided the face into three thirds: from hairline to the eyebrows, from there to the tip of the nose, and from herewith to the chin and analyzed differences and changes from the youthful to the aging profile. Leonardo was maybe the most fascinating artist and scientist of the Renaissance, some say until today, and defined "divine proportions," which he had studied and refined in the Vitruvian man, creating his own famous version of it, for example, by adding the circle and changing leg and arm positions (Fig. 1).

Leonardo's Vitruvian man now is omnipresent; that is, on the Italian 1-Euro coin, on insurance logos, and more. Leonardo's works are collected in the so-called Codex Atlanticus

- a masterpiece so large that it resembled an atlas, and was thus so named. The Codex Atlanticus is still preserved in the Library Ambrosiana in Milan, Italy. In it, multiple sketches and drawings are composed, trying to express nature in mathematical formulas, since Leonardo was constantly seeking answers to fundamental questions—he also calls for the existence of "10 nasal types": "If you want to acquire facility for bearing in mind the expression of a face, first make yourself familiar with a variety of [forms of] several heads, eyes, noses, mouths, chins and cheeks and necks and shoulders: And to put a case.

Noses are of ten types: straight, bulbous, hollow, prominent above or below the middle, aquiline, regular, flat, round or pointed. These hold good as to profile. In full face they are of eleven types; these are equal thick in the middle, thin in the middle, with the tip thick and the root narrow, or narrow at the tip and wide at the root; with the nostrils wide or narrow, high or low, and the openings wide or hidden by the point; and you will find an equal variety in the other details; which things you must draw from nature and fix them in your mind."

In the La Specola Museum in Florence, Italy, there are multiple wax models and drawings of Leonardo da Vinci preserved, showing his unique curiosity as a scientist and artist. It opened in 1775 for the common public and is to date still one of the largest scientific museums in Europe, containing some 3.5 million preserved animals, among which 5,000 are under constant display, and bird skeletons. There are also the largest collections of anatomical wax models visible, of which many have been made or inspired da Vinci himself. Leonardo da Vinci also illustrated the mathematical masterpiece by Luca Pacioli "De Divina Proportione"- on divine proportion. He underlined his mathematical knowledge by this collaboration, as he himself was not allowed to study at a university as an illegitimate child, and thus acquired his knowledge by merely asking and studying with other artists and scientists.

Jacques Joseph, one of the fathers of modern rhinoplasty, used the da Vinci drawing "Portrait of a Young Woman in Profile" to describe the nasofacial angle, which he called "profile angle."(fig-2) Also Michelangelo in the Renaissance times extensively studied the facial profile in his famous pictures of satyrs and characteristic men.

Fig. 2 Profilometer of Jacques Joseph.

Fig. 3 Leonello d'Este by Pisanello

Albrecht Dürer (1471–1528) was also interested in the proportions of the human body and especially the facial profile and published 10 sketches of human facial proportions in 1522. His characteristic and expressive facial portrayals are renowned . In the neoclassic times, the German sculptor and artist von Schadow tried to (Fig. 3) Leonello d'Este by Pisanello, calculate the average measurements of the nose by manuallymeasuring angles of pieces of art—by assuming statues and paintings would depict perfect bodies. The antic interpretations of Polemon or Adamantios, the group of authors' names "Pseudo-Aristoteles," tried to assign characteristic traits to special morphisms and body forms, and searched for medieval ages continue those ideas.

Humana Physiognomia, published in 1586 by Giambattista della Porta(1541–1615), is one of the most famous of these works (Fig. 4). It influenced the research of Charles Le Brun (1619–1690), who was the second-most influential artist of his time after Louis IV. It marks substantial aspects also of the anthropology of Petrus Camper (1722–1789), a Dutch anatomist; Johann Kaspar Lavater (1741–1801), a Swiss physiognomist; and Louis-Pierre Baltard (1764–1846), a French painter and architect (Fig. 5).

Comparing human and animal skeleton in detail, some erroneous doctrines emerged at that time, misinterpreting the great variety of skulls of the human family and their relationship to character and intelligence. Representative for those days, Camper postulated that when the brain is large, the face and sensory organs are small arguing that the relationship of the intellect and the face should be directly inverse.

Fig. 4 Giambattista della Porta (1535–1615). Human and sheep. De Humana Physiognomia, 1586.

Fig. 5 Louis-Pierre Baltard (1764–1846). Human and eagle (by Charles Le Brun).

Ethnic Influences

The influence of ethnic differences in the aesthetic judgment has been shown by many authors. Langlois and coworkers underline the cultural-specific standards of beauty and that faces least deviating from the normal cultural standard are the paragon of facial beauty. As a matter of fact, facial characteristics and the taste of beauty differ mostly in the area of the nose, the eye, the mouth, and the ear. The most prominent traits of the Asian face are the epicanthal fold and the under-projected dorsum of a small nose with flared nostrils.

Fig. 6 Bust of Ramses II, called "The YoungerMemnon," 19th Dynasty_1250 BCE.

On the contrary, Caucasians present the so-called double eyelid contour with deeper-set eyes, higher or overprojected nose often and a rather elongated narrow facial shape. The typical African face may be characterized by its wide, under-projected nose, the thicker dark brown or black skin, and full upper and lower lips. Facing ancient profiles, many of the previously described traits may be recognized, each representing its own identity. So busts of the ancient race of the Copts as of Amenophis the second, also known as Younger Memnon (Fig. 6), show facial features as a sloping forehead, full eyes stretching toward the temple, enlarged nostrils, elevated ear, and full lips which contrast interestingly with the later Greek and Roman facial profile and even to trends of the modern world.

When considering ethnical differences in the measurements of a facial profile, there are various investigations found in the current literature. Sheridan and colleagues used the Fourier shape analysis in the quantification of facial profiles of 121 healthy dental students and investigated thedifferences between racial groups. A comparison of multiple means tests revealed significant differences ($p < 0.05$) in the third-order Fourier harmonic (vertex projection) between the Asian group and the Anglo-Celtic, Eastern European, and Western European groups. Differences correlated with convexity in the lower third of the face, which was demonstrated by Fourier reconstruction.[8]

The physical anthropologists in earlier days worked with dry skull. Keith and Campion studied human facial growth from childhood to adulthood, using immature and mature skulls and 32 living individuals. Hellman made over 45,000 measurements of external dimensions of the face after studying 705 males and 988 females ranging from 3 to 22 years of age.

He concluded that, "the infant face is transformed into that of the adult not only by increases in size, but by changes in proportion and adjustment in position as well." Broadbent instrumented a longitudinal study of over 4000 subjects in 1929 at Case Reserve University in Ohio. The findings were presented in the form of superimposed tracings of serial cephalograms made at several stages from 1 month to adulthood. This study is known as Bolton Brush growth study.

Behrents did an extensive adult follow-up research of subjects in the original Bolton study, analyzing 163 subjects in the age range of 17 to 83 years. He concluded that craniofacial size and shape changes continue past 17 years to the oldest ages studied. He summarized that significant sexual dimorphism existed: men are larger at all ages, they grow more, and their adult growth is more apt to persist along the same vectors of adolescent growth. On the other hand, women showed periods of increased rates of craniofacial growth, apparently related to the time of pregnancies.[9]

CHAPTER FIVE

CHILD FACE

In general, esthetic evaluation in children is more difficult than in adults because the development of the soft-tissue profile is influenced by skeletal growth, but facial esthetics is a primary area of concern starting at 6 years of age. From a clinical point of view, it is often too early to begin a treatment, but the quantification of the soft-tissue profile at this age could be useful from a prognostic and diagnostic point of view.[10]

Clinical features

The child has a high intellectual-like forehead without coarse eyebrow ridges, with prominent cheekbones, large and wideset eyes, and a flat face. It has a short nose, low nasal bridge, and a concave nasal profile. The face is vertically short because of small nasal part, still growing jaw bones and not yet established primary and secondary dentition. Whether a young child's head form is dolichocephalic or brachycephalic, the face itself appears more brachycephalic-like because it is still relatively wide and vertically short .

In a profile view, the most striking feature is lower jaw which is far retrusive than the face above. The general tendency seems to be for the mandible to grow from the more retruded to a less retruded position and this is usually true regardless of the individual facial type. The maxilla tends to be positioned in a forward direction much more slowly than does the mandible, resulting in a decrease in the convexity of the facial profile. This differential growth in an anterior direction determines the final facial type at the completion of growth .

Why Is There a Change in Profile?

i. *Differential Growth: Hard Tissue/Soft Tissue.*

According to Scammon's growth curve, different organs in the body grow at different times to a different amount at different rates.

i. *Cephalo-Caudal Gradient of Growth.*

There is an axis of increased growth extending from head towards the feet. This increased gradient of growth is evident even within the face. The cranium is proportionally larger than face during birth but, postnatally, face grows more than cranium. Similarly, the mandible grows more in amount and for longer duration than maxilla.

iii. *Function.*

In a child, nasal part of the face is underdeveloped because of overall small body and lung size at that stage. Correspondingly, respiratory function has low demands. The nasal part of the face and the pharyngeal space has to enlarge in response to increased demands on respiratory function imparted by increasing overall body and lung size. For the nasomaxillary space to enlarge, nasomaxillary complex has to grow out from beneath the anterior cranial base. Then both the jaws have to grow to accommodate erupting deciduous and subsequently permanent dentition and enlarging muscles of mastication. These factors impart a vertical height and a depth to the face.

Hard Tissue Profile Changes Forehead

The neurocranium grows earlier faster and to a much greater extent than facial complex. Cranial cavity completes 90% of its growth by 5 yrs of age. The young child's forehead is upright and bulbous. This region seems very large and high because the face beneath it is still relatively small. But in the following years the face enlarges much more so that the proportionate size of the forehead becomes reduced. Pneumatization of the frontal sinus is responsible for the supraorbital ridges becoming prominent and forehead becoming much more sloping.

Nasal Bone

The young child has small rounded nose that protrudes very little and is vertically quite short. The nasal bridge is quite low with the lateral bony wall of the nose being characteristically narrow and shallow. The whole nasal region of the infant is vertically shallow and the nasal floor lies close to the inferior orbital rim. The shape of the nasal bridge changes from concave to convex.

Maxilla and Mandible

Björk and Palling found that during the earlier teenage years, growth of the mandible exceeds that of the maxilla resulting in straightening of the profile and retroclination of the lower incisors which may be one of the reasons for the increase in lower arch crowding at that time.

Longitudinal studies on postpubertal growth are limited. Slightly smaller jaw length increases were noted by Sarnas and Solow between 21 and 26 years, Bishara et al. between 25 and 46 years, and by Bondevik between 22 and 33 years. Lewis et al. also showed that growth in the mandible and cranial base continues into the third decade.

Premaxilla

The anterior outline of the bony maxillary arch in the infant has a vertically convex topography. This is in contrast to the characteristic concavity this region develops in the adulthood. The alveolar bone in this area of the adult face is noticeably protrusive. Anterior contour of premaxilla is flat in infants; the differential remodeling process draws out this contour.

Age-Related Arch Width Changes

Bishara et al. found that for maxillary arch, intercanine width increases between 3 and 13 yrs by 6 mm but decreases by 1.7 mm between 13 and 45 yrs. On the other hand, intermolar width increases by 2 mm between 3 and 5 yrs and by 2.2 mm between 8 and 13 yrs but decreases by 1 mm by 45 yrs of age. There is a slight decrease in arch length with age because of uprighting of the incisors..

In mandibular arch, intercanine width increases between 3 and 13 yrs by 3.7 mm but decreases by 1.2 mm between 13 and 45 yrs. Intermolar width increases by 1.5 mm between 3 and 5 yrs and by 1 mm between 8 and 13 yrs but decreases by 1 mm by 45 yrs of age. There is a slight decrease in arch length with age because of uprighting of the incisors and loss of leeway space by the mesial movement of the first permanent molars.

Mandibular intercanine width, on the average, is established by 8 years of age, that is, after the eruption of the four incisors. After the eruption of the permanent dentition, the clinician should either expect no changes or a slight decrease in arch widths.

Anterior Facial Height

The increase in anterior face height is probably largely due to continued tooth eruption. In females, the slight increase in the maxillary/mandibular plane angle may contribute to the increase in anterior face height. Sarnas and Solow and Forsberg suggested that the major part of the anterior face height increase in the third decade takes place in the first half of the decade. However, Bondevik who reported a 1.0 mm increase in anterior face height between 22 and 33 years and Bishara et al.who found a 1.9 mm increase between 25 and 46 years refute this statement. Apparently, anterior face height increase continues well into the fourth decade.

Posterior Facial Height

In males, the posterior facial height increases by almost as much as the anterior face height. In females, the posterior face height does not increase significantly in contrast to the anterior face height. This accounts for the slight increase in the maxillary/mandibular plane angle. However, Bishara et al. found that anterior and posterior face heights increased by the same amount in females with no significant change in the mandibular plane angle from 25 to 46 years.

Chin

The chin is incompletely formed in the infant. The mandible of the young child is quite small and retrusive relative to the upper jaw. The anterior cranial fossa is developmentally precocious. Hence, the nasomaxillary complex is carried to a more protrusive position. The mandible, which articulates on the middle cranial fossae, is located more posteriorly. With continuing growth, the chin tends to assume forward position relative to the superior aspects of the skeletal face and the mandible grows from the more retruded to a less retruded position[11].

CHAPTER SIX

THE AGING FACE

Each person may have individual issues about what specific facial features are attractive or unattractive, they may disagree with people in other cultures about certain attributes of beauty, but much of what is considered attractive is shared across cultures. During past few years there was noticeable come back of researches on the human face morphological markers, face aging changes. There are made numerous studies focused on face attractiveness, face recognition, even connection between appearance and intelligence. Many scientists are interested in the factors that contribute to the attractiveness of the face, how someone's attractiveness affects others and their behavior and how it might improve or maintain facial attractiveness. Dentists, genetics, plastic surgeons, antropologists, forensic experts are trying to understand face changes during humans life and how enviromental and genetic factors changes our appearance. Aging is an inevitable process. Changes in the face secondary to aging are the most apparent. Facial aging is a dynamic process involving the aging of soft-tissue and bony structures.

The major forces responsible for facial aging include gravity, soft tissue maturation, skeletal remodeling, muscular facial activity, solar changes and changes in stomatognatic system. These factors can be classified into local and systemic.

The aging changes seen in the lower third of the face affect the lips, chin, lower cheeks and neck. Changes in dentition and absorption of maxillary and mandibular bone may result in an overall loss of height and volume. Aging across the mandibular border may be described by several mechanisms: fat atrophy, volume loss and loss of elasticity. These changes may result in the lower third of the face appearing smaller relative to the upper and middle thirds, straying from the ideal, approximately equal proportions.

Aging changes from the middle third of the face may contribute to this appearance, as nasal tip ptosis may create the appearance of a shortened upper lip. The constant effects of gravity combined with loss of elasticity in the tissue may allow for excess skin to drop off the mandible. Some authors say that volume loss, including soft and hard tissue is at least equally important as gravity in the pathogenesis of aging.

There are two ways by which face, and for that matter skin ages: internally and externally. Internal aging is what's commonly referred to as the "natural" aging process.

This type of aging occurs as human gets older and involves

- Collagen production slowing (collagen contributes to skin's fi rmness)
- Elastin production decreases (elastin contributes to skin's elasticity)
- Fat cells begin to disappear (which can lead to sagging skin)
- Your skin losing its ability to retain moisture
- Frown lines appearing due to small muscle contractions
- Dead skin cells not being shed as quickly
- Slightly less turnover of new skin cells.

Some aspects of aging are fairly uncontrollable, and these are largely based on hereditary factors. Other factors are somewhat controllable and are largely the result of exposure to the elements and harmful habits.

The Environment

A number of factors contribute to and in many instances accelerate the natural aging process. Prolonged or frequent exposure to environmental agents such as sunlight (ultraviolet radiation) and wind or arid climates can cause skin, particularly the more delicate skin of the face, to age prematurely. In addition to the photo damage caused by sunlight, which dries and destroys the cells and underlying structure of the skin, exposure to the sun gives the skin a furrowed, thickened appearance and hastens the development of wrinkles, especially around the eyes as a product of squinting . Aridity and wind likewise dehydrate the skin, contributing to the formation of wrinkles, but the effect of ultraviolet radiation from the sun on the facial tissues by far exceeds these agents in effect. Chronic sun exposure can result in numerous changes in human skin, particularly on the face, changes in photoaging include wrinkling, elastosis, actinic keratoses, irregular pigmentation.With continued exposure to the sun and other elements, the color and texture of the face can change, becoming blotchy, yellowish, and leathery, with loose, inelastic, hyperpigmented skin. Blood vessels lying close to the surface of the skin may become prominent as networks called spider veins, adding to the skin's overall mottled and blotched appearance.

The potential detrimental effects of tobacco smoking have been widely cited. Smoking is an important determinant of macroscopic skin ageing and wrinkling in older subjects. This evidence suggests that skin ageing does not clearly provide an objective measure of cumulative ultraviolet exposure, and caution should be exercised before it is used in this way. Important characteristics of the aging skin are elastosis and telangiectasia. Although some studies shows what role of smoking in the skin wrinkling is minor.

Orthodontic Treatment

In some cases, variations in the appearance of the face can be explained by changes in the position of the teeth to orthodontic treatment.Though such treatment is mainly performed on children and teenagers, it is not uncommon in adults and may impart a greater change in appearance in these older individuals, especially as it may be used more to achieve aesthetic results. It is important that at the aging human changes lip line during speech or smiling. Mandibular tooth display in the rest position increases significantly. Upper lip length increases significantly by almost 4 mm in older subjects, whereas upper lip elevation did not change significantly. The significant increasing lip coverage of the maxillary teeth indicates that the effects of age should be included in orthodontic treatment planning .

The dynamic measures indicate that the muscles ability to create a smile decreases with increasing age. Most aesthetic dental work involves the extraction of premolars and molars in the upper or lower jaws. The main soft tissue differences between the patients at the end of treatment are a more retruded lower lip and a more pronounced lower labial sulcus in those patients subjected to extraction. Removal of the wisdom teeth in the maxilla will cause the face to appear narrower, removing premolars from the mandible and pulling the remaining lower teeth together by means of orthodontics can markedly alter the profile of the face and lessen the effect of an inherited dominant chin. Some aesthetic treatments of this nature, especially those involving surgery and an associated restructuring of the face, may alter an individual's facial appearance.

Untreated dental or surgical problems may also result in distinctively altered facial characteristics. An individual with an open bite, for instance, may compensate for the situation with muscular action in the chin area; over time this condition will create grooves and wrinkles in that region. The relative changes in the position of the lips, nose, and chin, cause the lips to appear more retrusive at 46 years of age. These changes should be taken into consideration when orthodontists are considering various treatment and retention options for their adult patients.

Teeth Loss

Tooth loss is an undesirable entity which occurs due to physical injury or disease. The condition of missing teeth is medically termed as edentulism or anodontia. Loss of teeth is frequently associated with periodontal disease in older adults. Aging alone does not lead to critical loss of periodontal attachment in healthy elderly persons, older patients retain their natural teeth for longer and clinical picture consists of normal age changes in combination with pathological and iatrogenic effects.

The effects of aging on periodontal tissues intensify teeth and bone loss in elderly patients with periodontitis. Bone remodeling is linked to the functional need of an individual's body where there is a need for bony tissue, it is deposited; where it is not needed, it is resorbed.

Depending on the loads and stresses placed on the skeletal system, nutrition, and other factors affecting the individual, the density and thickness of bone will vary. When a human loses teeth, the demand for support in the bone surrounding the teeth will be decreased. This leads to a resorption of bone in those not active areas, a process which is more pronounced in the upper jaw than in the lower jaw. The presence of less bony tissue in the upper jaw decreases the height of the face and causes the lower jaw to appear more prominent. Reduction of facial height, most marked in the maxilla and mandible, and strongly correlated with loss of teeth.

The loss of support tissues in the face leads to the formation of wrinkles and affects the muscles of the lower face, which must compensate for the absence of teeth, cheeks can appear hollow. When teeth are lost from the lateral areas of the jaw, there can be a narrowing of the face as well as a hollowing of the cheeks; anterior tooth loss will produce a concave profile. Total loss of the teeth will affect the density and thickness of the jaw bones, resulting reduced size of the jaw area and foreshortened facial appearance. In this way tooth loss has a significant effect on both the underlying skeletal proportions of the face and the overlying soft tissues. Therefore total face height ratio remains stable throughout adulthood among individuals who have relatively intact dentitions, or anterior face height may increase due to teeth eruption.

Replacement of the natural teeth with dentures may inhibit the continued resorption of bone in the upper and lower jaws to some extent, but a change in the volume of the bone tissue in the jaws will usually be visible. With increasing age and due to periodontal disease the body resorbs much of the bone tissue composing the jaws, causing the gums to recede and the roots of the teeth to become visible the expression which can be used to describe an aged appearance. The wearing of the occlusal surfaces of the teeth over time leads to the decreasing vertical height of the face, and also can cause flattening and remodeling of the temporomandibular joint as a product of arthritis. Bruxism is one of the most prevalent, complex, and destructive dental functional disorders. The affects of bruxism and clenching become increasingly apparent as patients live longer. Many aging patients have worn their teeth to the degree that they cannot chew properly, and the teeth are painful.

Remodeling

Throughout life, bone tissue is continuously being formed, removed, and replaced. The bones of the face retain the capacity for remodeling at any age. During youth, particularly before the age of twenty and with peak velocity at puberty, the deposition, growth, and modelling of bony tissues predominates. This sequential, chronological process is physically evident in the changing shape, height, and facial structure of males and females with entry into early adulthood. The facial skeleton appears to rotate such that the frontal bone moves anteriorly and inferiorly while the maxilla moves posteriorly and superiorly.

This rotation causes bony angles to become more acute and likely has an effect on the position of overlying soft tissues. These changes appear to be more dramatic in women. The mandible bone ageing and osteoporosis differs sufficiently from postcranial skeletal sites it would be unwise to extrapolate from findings in the jaw to the circumstances elsewhere. By age 28 the formation and growth of the human skeletal system in most individuals is complete and physical changes occurring after this developmental milestone primarily involve bone remodeling and resorption, tissue degeneration.

Gender

Gender differences in health, socioeconomic status, and social resources persist into advanced old age and result in variations in life trajectories and responses to the challenges of longevity. Demographic changes have forced gerontologists to focus attention on the gender based character of population aging. The aging process of male and female faces share many common features, attention to the particular differences in the aging man is warranted. Gender differences in the male face include the presence of facial hair, increased facial vascularity, increased thickness, increased sebaceous content, hormonal influences, and potentially differing rates of fat and bone absorption during the life cycle. Women tend to develop more and deeper wrinkles in the perioral region than men; their skin contains a significantly smaller number of appendages than men.

Women who look young for their age have large lips, avoid sunexposure and possess genetic factors that protect against the development of gray hair and skin wrinkles. High social status, low depression score and being married are associated with a younger look, but the strength of the associations varies between genders. Using literature search, we found more factors which can affect face changes, like a nutrition, genetic anomalies, internal diseases and human races, but we excluded these factors because of lack of common data. Factors like plastic surgery excluded, because we were interested in aging, not affected by medical procedures.[12]

The facial skeleton is generally believed to expand continuously throughout life. This is reflected in the progressive increase in certain facial anthropometric measurements with age such as the nasion-to-anterior nasal spine and the facial width. The fact that certain areas of the facial skeleton also undergo resorption with aging is not well appreciated or even accepted. For example, it has been thought that maxillary retrusion of the maxilla does not occur with aging in the fully dentate patient. However, contrary to this view, recent evidence clearly demonstrates that aging of the maxilla is primarily one of bone resorption.

Selective bone resorption in the facial skeleton is not without precedent. Most notably, in the process of differential growth, areas of bone resorption occur adjacent to areas of bone deposition. Differential growth enables the infant skull to assume the proportions of the adult form. This process continues to remodel the fully dentate mature, facial bone and alters the craniofacial morphology into one that is instantly recognizable as an aged skull. Despite this, the concept that specific areas of the adult facial skeleton are susceptible to resorption remains controversial. Some authors have argued that the skeleton itself undergoes minimal changes with aging and that ongoing aging merely unmasks the underlying skeletal structure

Selective resorption occurs in specific areas of the adult facial bone. Contrary to conventional beliefs, remodelling of the facial skeleton occurs unabated regardless of the state of the dentition, although the loss of dentition significantly accelerates bony resorption of the maxilla and mandible.

Periorbital Region

The orbital aperture increases with age, in both area and width. Resorption is, however, uneven and site specific. The superomedial and inferolateral aspects of the orbital rim, in particular, recede more, although the changes occur at different rates (Fig. 1). The inferolateral orbital rim changes manifest earlier, by middle age, whereas in the superomedial quadrant, recession may be noted only in old age. The inferomedial quadrant of the orbit also has a tendency to recede in old age, especially in males. In contrast, the central part of the superior and inferior orbital rims is more stable, with little if any resorption occurring with age. Pessa found no significant changes in the orbital angle (superior-to-inferior midorbital rim points on the lateral view) with aging, indicating that either the orbital rims do not recede or that one does not recede more rapidly than the other. Mendelson et al directly measured the lengths of the orbital roof and floor with aging (at the mid axis of each orbit) and found no significant changes in these distances with aging, indicating that the central portion of the superior and inferior orbital rims do not recede with aging.

Fig. 1- Orbital aging. The superomedial and inferolateral aspects of the orbit have the greatest tendency to resorb. This contributes to the stigmata of periorbital aging such as increased prominence of the medial fatpad, elevation of the medial brow, and lengthening of the lid cheek junction

Midface

The midface skeleton is formed by the maxilla in themedial and middle thirds and by the body and arch of the zygoma in the lateral third. Contrary to conventional orthodontic teaching, it has been clearly demonstrated recently that midface retrusion does occur with aging in dentulous patients. The rate of bony resorption in the midface, however, is not uniform. The maxilla is more susceptible to age-related loss than the zygoma.

Pessa measured the maxillary angle (superior-toinferior maxilla at the articulation of the inferior maxillary wing and alveolar arch) of young and old patients and demonstrated significant bone resorption with loss of projection of the maxilla. Shaw and Kahn similarly noted a significant reduction of the maxillary angle with aging (Fig. 2). Using a more precise approach to measurement with standardized parasagittal computed tomography (CT) slices through the midaxis of the orbit to measure the angle between the floor of the orbit and the anterior maxilla, Mendelson et al confirmed the important finding that the maxilla retrudes with aging and quantitated the changes. The maxillary angle decreased by about 10 between young (age < 30 years) and old (age > 60 years) individuals.

Fig. 2 The piriform (piriform angle) and the maxilla (maxillary angle) significantly recede with aging, from youth (left) to old age (right)

Perinasal Changes

The characteristics of the aging nose are well known and include the following key changes. The nose lengthens and the tip droops, with the collumella and the lateral crurae displacing posteriorly. Changes in the bony foundation that support the nose in youth, the paired nasal bone, and the ascending processes of the maxillae are responsible for many of the soft tissues changes seen in the nose with aging.

Shaw and Khan found that the piriform aperture, resembling the situation of the orbital aperture, enlarges with aging as the edges of the nasal bones recede with age. Similarly, bone loss is not uniform, with the greatest resorption occurring in the ascending process of the maxilla. The posterior displacement of the bone rim is greatest at the lower pyriform aperture, which is the critical area for support of the lateral crurae and the external nasal valves.

Pessa measured the length of the perpendicular line from the nasion to the pyriform on standardized lateral views of three-dimensional CT images and observed that the distance increases significantly with aging, indicating preferential bone loss in the lower part of the pyriform aperture (Fig. 3). This manifests clinically as posterior displacement of the alar base (relative to the fixed position of the medial canthus) (Fig. 4). Bone loss here contributes also to deepening of the nasolabial fold with age, which previously had been attributed solely to soft tissue laxity and descent. The anterior nasal spine also recedes with aging (although at a slower rate), and this reduced skeletal support contributes to retraction of the collumella, with downward tip rotation and apparent lengthening of the nose with aging.

Fig. 3 In youth, the piriform (P) lies anterior to the anterior lacrimal crest (A). With aging, the piriform comes to lie posterior to the anterior lacrimal crest as a result of selective bone resorption at the piriform (below)

Fig. 4 The loss of bone in the pyriform area weakens the support of the lateral crura. Deepening of the maxilla results in posterior positioning of the nasolabial crease and adjacent upper lip

Lower Face

The dentate mandible is assumed to expand continuously with aging. This was substantiated by two longitudinal studies. Pecora et al found that the length of the mandible increases with age for both genders based on lateral cephalograms of 19 male and 20 female subjects.

Pessa et al, using frontal radiographs of eight males and eight females from the Bolton Brush Growth Study, found an increase in mandible width and height with increasing age.

The most recent study on aging of the mandible compared three-dimensional CT scans in a population of 120 young, middle-aged, and elderly subjects. In contrast to earlier studies, although certain measurements increased significantly with aging, some measurements contracted. There were no significant changes in the bigonial width and ramus breadth with aging. Whereas the mandibular angle increased, the ramus height and mandibular body height and length decreased. These findings contradict the earlier studies, which suggest that the mandible expands continuously with age. This may be related to the measurement of normal growth in young subjects who have not yet reached skeletal maturity, inadvertently giving a result that the mandible is larger than in the old-age group.

For example, in the longitudinal study of Pessa et al, the age range of the female young group was 5–17 years. Comparing these young subjects with mature subjects would most likely result in the latter appearing larger, thereby giving the impression of continuous expansion with aging.

Shaw et al compared subject groups in three age ranges: 20–40, 41–64 years, and older than 64 years (i.e., all subjects had attained full maturity). These standard parameters, based on linear measurements, will fail to detect in-between areas of reduced skeletal projection such as the prejowl region of the mandible that develops into an area of relative concavity and contributes to the appearance of jowls. Jowls appear at a younger age in patients with microgenia because of the relatively inadequate skeletal support in this area.

More than 40 years ago, Enlow followed the growth of the facial skeleton longitudinally from infancy to young adulthood by means of serial cephalometrograms and noted that the entire face becomes longer vertically, deeper in the anterior posterior plane, and wider in the transverse dimension. The following specific changes occur with growth: increasing protrusion of the glabella; expansion of the supraorbital ridges; lateral translation of the orbits; increase in the depth and lateral expansion of the cheeks; increase in length, width, and vertical dimensions of the nose; and increase in vertical height in the occlusal region associated with increased chin prominence.

Enlow's findings formed the basis for the widely accepted teaching that craniofacial growth is one of continuous expansion throughout life. The traditional concepts of facial aging revolve around the theme of changes occurring in the soft tissues, with atrophic laxity leading to tissue descent. The areas most affected by reduced skeletal prominence correspond to those areas of the face that manifest the most prominent stigmata of aging (Fig. 5).

Fig. 5 The darker areas are those of the greatest bone loss. The stigmata of aging, manifested by the facial soft tissues, corresponds with the areas of weakened skeletal support.

In the medial aspect of the upper lid, the brow position is noted to ascend paradoxically with aging, exaggerating the drooped look of the lateral brow. The medial orbital fat pad also becomes more prominent with age, possibly associated with the recession of the superomedial orbital rim. The midcheek manifests the most complex soft tissue changes with aging. The development of the tear-trough deformity, malar mounds, and prominent nasolabial fold and groove may to a significant degree be attributed to the loss of projection of the maxilla with aging.

The changes over the lower face are less complex, with the jowl appearing more prominent in relation to the area of reduced skeletal support in the prejowl area of the mandible. In the midcheek, weakness of skeletal support medially contributes to the 'tear- trough deformity'(Fig-6), and over the malar segment laterally, the changes manifest as malar mounds. Additionally, the major loss of bone projection of the maxilla that contributes to the edge of the pyriform aperture, particularly inferiorly, results in less support of the alar base and upper lip part of the nasolabial groove

(Fig-6) -"tear-trough deformity"

Whereas the traditional focus of nasolabial correction has always been on the descent of the heavy fold and the redraping of this from above, it may be more logical to correct the depth of the upper lip position secondary to skeletal changes. The question of why certain sites are more prone to bony resorption than others has been the subject of little discussion.

The maxilla is the bone that undergoes the most dramatic resorption with aging, the consequences of which are seen in the aging mid cheek. The maxilla differs in origin and function from the other bones that make up the orbital rim, being a bone of dental origin. In youth, the maxilla expands to accommodate the growing secondary dentition, which develops within the bone. Eruption of the secondary dentition results in a major reduction of the maxilla's volume, especially in its lower part. It is reasonable to speculate that the reverse, i.e., a lack of stress, may be a factor contributing to bone losses in these areas.

It is interesting then to note that the sites identified as areas prone to bony resorption in the facial skeleton correspond to the more mobile part of the face during animation, especially the obicularis oculi covering the lateral brow, the lateral orbital crow's feet areas, and the inferolateral orbital rim. The mobility required for the function of these regions is structurally associated with a less ligamentous fixation of the soft tissues to the bone. Hence, the attachment of the muscles and ligament to the bone in these areas is attended by little stress.

It is reasonable to speculate that the opposite, a lack of stress, may be a factor contributing to bone losses in these areas. Some people inherently "age better" than others. These individuals can be recognized in youth because they have a more attractive face with a strong skeletal structure, as evidenced by the presence of youthful bony features that provide good support to the overlying soft tissues. These features include a prominent supraorbital bar, a strong cheekbone, and a prominent jaw line. Because these individuals innately have youthful bony contours, they start off "high on the curve" of bony support so that it takes longer for the bone loss of aging to manifest clinically.BConversely, people with poor facial skeletal support never have the ideal contours of youth and start off lower down the curve, and many appear old for their age, even in their 20's. They are effectively predisposed to manifest aging changes prematurely.

Conclusion

The facial skeleton has a profound effect on an individual's appearance. A defining characteristic of youth is good skeletal structural support. Facial aging results from a combination of soft tissue and bony changes, with bone loss in specific areas of the facial skeleton contributing significantly to the features of the aging face. This comprehensive review highlights the specific areas known to resorb with aging. It is conceptually important to appreciate that in most individuals with premature aging, the facial skeleton can be inherently inadequate. Accordingly, the changes in the facial skeleton that result from the aging process must be addressed to obtain a natural-appearing facial rejuvenation.[13]

CHAPTER SEVEN

MALE VS FEMALE

Modern society has placed a strong emphasis on physical attractiveness. facial esthetics is an important attribute upon which opinions and perceptions of characterability are conceived. Facial symmetry and average proportion in women were found to be significant facial features that influence the selection process by men, whereas enhanced secondary male sexual characteristics were the primary feature that affected women's choices. [14]

Sexual dimorphism

Sexual dimorphism relates to the recognition of two sexes per species and the phenotypic expression of multi-factorial differences at the chromosomal, gonadal, hormonal and behavioral levels. These differences also have the evolutionary significance, and might be adaptations for mate choice. There are known gender differences in facial characteristics. The majority of facial features containing secondary sexual traits develop or increase in size at puberty under the influence of sex hormones. For example, males have more pronounced noses, brows and frontal regions, more prominent chins and larger jaws compared with females.

Some studies suggest that women have bigger eyes, smaller noses and thinner lips. The perception of facial attractiveness is, among other factors, influenced by facial symmetry. Symmetry, sexual dimorphism and averageness are good candidates for biologically based standards of beauty. Average faces follow average trait values for a specific population. Averageness is conditioned not only racially, but also ethnically within the race. The symmetry is more pronounced in females, because beauty has a larger role in the male evolutionary principles of female mate selection. Some studies found a positive correlation between masculinity and symmetry in male faces, while others failed to confirm these findings.[15]

Sexual dimorphism of the adult human face has been confirmed in many studies using various methodological approaches. Methods of traditional morphometrics mostly found that the size of the average male face is greater compared to the female face. The degree of sexual dimorphism in various facial dimensions is not uniform and depends on the specific part of the face, loading, social status, ethnicity, age, nutrition and other factors. In other words, the human face is population specific. In addition to this finding, the large adult faces have a different shape in comparison with smaller faces, i.e., they display static allometry.

Ageing and development of sexual dimorphism

According to Koudelova´ et al, it is the facial form, not shape, that more closely reflects the development of facial sexual dimorphism during puberty. In their study, the intersexual difference of facial form increased with age, which corresponds to the results of Ferrario et al.,who used a similar methodology. Sexual dimorphism of facial meshes was evaluated in detail, however, disregarding age. Unfortunately, comparative data for different age intervals could not be found. Significant sexual dimorphism of adult facial size and shape separately on the basis of landmark data was detected in another work. Similar results for young adults were obtained on the basis of the Euclidean distance matrix, where sexual dimorphism was more evident in the lower third of the face.

Sex-differences in various facial parts

When focusing on sex-differences in overall facial morphology and in various facial parts during ageing, the differences were observed both in form and shape. Generally, the female facial form became more round, while the male form varied from an oval to rectangular shape with age and was overall larger than female ones. It is a widely accepted fact that males have an extended period of growth. Therefore, they form more prominent facial features, whereas females have an attenuated growth, retaining more juvenile characteristics, though it is still not clear if craniofacial sex differences are due to the differences in the rate of ageing per se, or sexual dimorphism, or shifts in hormonal levels.

In the upper third of the face, the greatest levels of sexual dimorphism were found in the region of the eyebrow ridges, which was closely related with craniofacial morphology. Additionally, males and females differ in the rate and extent of facial bone changes with ageing. Males had noticeably more protruded eyebrow ridges in all age categories with respect to form. In association with the more prominent supraorbital part of the forehead, the eyes were situated deeper in males. A possible explanation is that the sinus enlargement in conjunction with size differences in certain areas of the orbit might cause this difference in the prominence of the glabella and eyebrow ridges. The shape differences in this region are dependent on age. The more pronounced male eyebrow ridges in young adults were not found in the eldest age category, and it seems that with age, the shape differences in this region diminish.

In the middle third of the face, the loss of convexity in both sexes is evident with increasing age. Similarly, Bishara et al. observed a decrease in facial convexity during young adulthood (between 25 and 45 years of age). Sex-differences in facial features were mostly evident in the cheeks and nose. The cheeks were more protruded in females, which corresponds to a generally greater amount of facial (buccal) fat in females. On the other hand, males had flatter cheeks in all age categories, probably due to their wider frontal and zygomatic processes. The most distinctive differences were observed in the nasal region. The nose length and nasal protrusion tended to be larger in males for the entire observed period.

In the young adults, the sex-differences were the most evident in the larger columella and tip of the nose. With increasing age (and especially in the eldest age category), the male nose became much wider in alar wings, which is connected with the overall widening of the face. According to Zankl et al, the nose continues to grow throughout the life because it is formed from cartilage that does not reach a definite length in early adulthood, such as bony structures. The changes in the shape of the nose during ageing showed distinct differences compared to the ageing of the nasal form. Although the differences in facial shape were significant in all age categories, we observed a decrease in sex differences in the shape of the nose. The shape of the nose in the eldest category may be influenced by pyriform remodelling and maxillary resorption, which affected the repositioning of the alar base and led to the similarity in nose shape and the decrease in the nasolabial angle in both sexes from mid to late adulthood.

The facial features in the lower third were mainly associated with an overall larger protrusion and prolongation of this part in males, both in form and shape (in agreement with). The areas between the nasolabial folds and upper and lower lips were larger in males in the first two categories, while in the eldest category, they were significantly reduced. This finding was reported in some other studies and can probably be attributed to the loss of elasticity of soft tissues of subcutaneous fat and muscle volume. In Bishara et al.'s study, the retrusion of both lips was described in much younger age categories (from 25 to 45 years of age). On the other hand, according to Rosati et al, no significant age or sex related differences in the average lip curvature were detected. The lip curvature variability was significantly greater in the young than in the aged subjects.

Allometry

Static allometry is defined as the relationship between size and shape within a single age stage, usually in adults. Parallel allometric trajectories suggest that similar developmental processes regulate growth in males and females, whereas divergent growth trajectories represent the sex-specific regulation of growth.

The allometric trajectory of elder males and its direction was related not only to sexual dimorphism but also to ageing morphological changes, the faces of the eldest males had an older appearance if they were larger. This may be because larger male faces with bigger soft tissues had a more apparent loss of muscle volume, subcutaneous fat and dehydration in the elder age category. On the other hand, this conclusion is contrary to other studies where females showed greater age changes, and the authors suggest that this was due to the effects of menopause.

Conclusion

We conclude that sex and age have a significant influence on the shape and form of the adult human face. The average male face of any age was larger than the average female face of the corresponding age. Ageing changes were similar in both sexes, although the female trajectory was considerably shorter. In addition to the increased visibility of skin folds and wrinkles, the female face during ageing became more rounded, while the male face transformed from an oval to a rectangular shape. Female faces underwent a less pronounced transformation during ageing and also tended to decrease in size more rapidly than the male faces. Sexual dimorphism of foreheads, eyebrow ridges, nose including the region under the upper lip,the mandible region and cheeks decreased with age.[16]

CHAPTER EIGHT

FACIAL TYPES

Facial type assessment is in many aspects crucial for the planning and prognosis of orthodontic treatment. Facial morphology is related to factors such as volume and shape of pharyngeal airspace, anatomy of masticatory muscles, dentoalveolar anatomy and occlusion type. Moreover, the facial pattern indicates the direction of growth of the craniofacial complex and must be taken into consideration when selecting the orthodontic biomechanics.[17]

The description of the dentofacial relationships of persons with normal and abnormal facial morphology is one of the most frequently addressed subjects in the orthodontic literature. This wealth of knowledge has consistently pointed to the large variation that exists in each population evaluated. As a result, many attempts have been made to describe the range of normal variation of the human face and design a system that identifies the various facial types. It is assumed that such a classification would be of value in the diagnosis and treatment planning of different craniofacial and dental discrepancies.

A facial-body type classification was presented by Salzmann using Kretschemer's description of somatic types These types were divided into

1. leptosomatic--long and slender with a facial height of similar proportions,
2. pyknic--short and squat with a face more broad and less high, and
3. the athletic somatic type characterized by a well-developed square mandible.[18]

Historic review

Prior to the interest of dentists and orthodontic specialists in facial balance, artists had often accurately described the variations of human physiognomy. A. Diirer, by modifying only some coordinates, had shown the contrast resulting between a convex and a concave profile or between a broad and a narrow face. Santayana, writing on the "sense of beauty," played a game of mismatching facial components of the same size and producing disproportionate profiles. Anthropologists put these initial attempts on a more scientific basis by measuring either the skulls or the soft tissues of the face and deriving types associated with racial variations. Following these earlier classifications, the development of medical knowledge suggested that perhaps some correlation exists between the facial pattern and certain predominant functions.

It was along this line of thought that Sheldonle established somatotypes or constitutional types on the basis of the predominant traits of endomorphy, mesomorphy, and ectomorphy. With the advent of roentgenographic cephalometry, the interest in the variability of facial patterns was renewed with a shift of emphasis toward their association with malocclusions. Bjork, Down, Graber, Lindegard, Sassouni, Ricketts, and Muller have described specific findings of skeletal imbalances associated predominantly with defined classes of malocclusion. Most of the descriptions, however, have been incomplete in the sense that they were centered on the profile or were based on only one dimension of space. Furthermore, the nomenclature, far from being standardized, added to the confusion.[19]

FACIAL TYPE

The facial height to width ratio (Facial index) gives the overall facial type, such as 'long' or 'short' or 'square' face. The proportionate facial height to width ratio is 1.35:1 for males and 1.3:1 for females. Bizygomatic facial width, measured from the most lateral point of the soft tissue overlying each zygomatic arch (zygion), is approximately 70% of vertical facial height. In addition, bitemporal width, measured from the most lateral point on each side of the forehead, is 80–85% of bizygomatic width. Bigonial width, measured from the soft tissue overlying the most lateral point of each mandibular angle (soft tissue gonion), is usually 70–75% of bizygomatic width.

The basic shape of the face when viewed from the frontal aspect can be one of the following

- Square
- Tapering
- Square tapering
- Ovoid

The lateral profile of an individual can be any one of the following

- Straight
- Convex
- Concave

FACIAL SYMMETRY

The face must also be examined for bilateral symmetry, bearing in mind that a small degree of asymmetry is present in most individuals and essentially normal. The facial midline can be constructed using two main landmarks. The mid-philtrum of the upper lip (Cupid's bow) will be in the midline of the face, except in exceptional circumstances, eg cleft lip. A line joining this point to the mid-glabellar region (glabella), midway between the eyebrows, forms the facial midline.

In the symmetrical face, this line will extend to the mid-point of the chin. The presence of a cant in the transverse occlusal plane may be assessed in relation to the interpupillary line with the patient biting on a wooden spatula, either in the incisor/canine region or the premolar/molar region. In the absence of a maxillary cant and/ or vertical/ orbital dystopia, the transverse occlusal plane should be parallel to the interpupillary line.[20]

Graber classified the individuals according to their facial types into:-

- The dolichocephalic individuals who have long and narrow faces and relatively narrow dental arches.
- The brachycephalic individuals who have very broad and relatively short faces and broad, round dental arches.
- Mesocephalic individuals who fit somewhere in between these two figures (fig-1)[21]

Figure 1. Dolicho-, brachy- and mesocephalic facial types; below, the most likely dental arch form that goes with each facial type

Simon, a German orthodontist, presented his classification of facial profiles as a part of a system of diagnosis and treatment for orthodontic cases. The primary objective of Simon's work was to achieve a scientifically correct diagnosis of facial anomalies in order that a proper type of orthodontic treatment might be instituted, the objective of the treatment being to bring all cases as near to the ideal or norm as possible.

The Simon classification is based upon relationship of anthropologic landmarks. The landmarks used may he explained briefly as follows :

- Cheilion

    - Corner of mouth

- Orbitale

    - The lowest point of the bony orbit; may be readily palpated and marked on the living subject. It is approximately below the pupil of the eye.

- Tragion

    - The rounded eminence anterior to the external auditory meatus, the superior border of which is approximately on the level with the superior margin of the external auditory meatus

- Gnathion

-The lowest and most anterior part on the body of the mandible .

- Gonion

-The angle of the mandible at the junction between the body and the ramus.

- Nasion

-Taken at the deepest point at the bridge of the nose actually it is the junction between the frontal and nasal bones at the nasofrontal suture.

- Subnasion

    - Point of junction between the nasal septum and the upper lip.

- Eye ear plane

-The plane passing through orbital points and the tragion. This is comparable to the Frankfort plane

- Orbital plane

    - A plane passing through the orbital points at right angles to the eye-ear plane

- Nasion line

  - A line dropped from the nasion running parallel to the orbital plane.

The classification proposed by Simon consists of five major groups:

- Norm Or Normal
- Protractions
- Retractions
- Attractions
- Abstractions.

Protractions and retractions are primarily horizontal cleviations from the normal whereas the attractions and abstractions are vertical deviations from the normal. Protractive and retractive groups are subdivided into maxillary, mandibular, and maxillomandibular (bimaxillary) types.

The mandibular retractive group are further sub grouped into

- Lower alveolar retraction
- Vertical mandibular retraction
- Horizontal mandibular retraction
- Total mandibular retraction (fig. 2) .

Fig – 2

THE NORM OR NORMAL TYPE

The norm as proposed by Simon is a straight or flat profile type with the orbital plane passing through the cheilion and the gnathion, the subnasion lying between the orbital plane and a line dropped from the nasion parallel to the orbital plane. The face is composed of equal thirds, that is, the distance from the hair- line to the nasion and the distance from the nasion to the subnasion and the distance from the subnasion to the gonion are approximately equal in length. Also, the distance from gnathion to gonion is approximately equal to the distance front gonion to tragion (Fig. 3).

Fig – 3

PROTRACTION

A maxillary protraction exists when the subnasion lies anterior to the nasion line, all other landmarks being normal. A mandibular protraction exists where the gnathion lies anterior to the orbial plane, all other landmarks being equal. A bimaxillary protraction exists when the subnasion lies anterior to the nasion line and the gnathion lies anterior to the orbital plane, other landmarks being normal.

RETRACTION

A maxillary retraction exists when the subnasion lies close to or is posterior to the orbital plane, other landmarks being normal. Mandibular retraction exists when the gnathion is posterior to the orbital plane, other landmarks being normal. Bimaxillary retraction exists when the subnasion is close to or is posterior to the orbital plane and the gnathion is posterior to the orbital plane. In classifying individual cases, the relationship of the teeth, the alveolar process, and the body of both the maxilla and the mandible must be taken into consideration. Also, the relative length of the ramus to the of the mandible is of importance.

ATTRACTION

An attraction may be considered to exist when the distance from the subnasion to the gnathion is less than other facial thirds. The shortening of the lower third is primarily from the cheilion to the base of the mandible.

ABSTRACTION

An abstraction may be considered to exist when the distance from the sub nasion to the gnathion is greater than other facial thirds. The excessive length of the lower third being from cheilion to gnathion.[22]

FACIAL FORM

The relationship between the facial width and height has a strong influence on facial harmony. The proportional relationship between the width and height is more important than absolute values in establishing the overall facial type. When evaluating facial form, the overall body build of the individual (corporofacial relationship) should be considered (ie, short and stocky vs long and thin). The height-to-width proportion (trichion to menton:bizygomatic width) is 1.3:1 for females and 1.35:1 for males. The bigonial width should be approximately 30% less than the bizygomatic dimension, and the width and shape of the chin should form a harmonious part of the overall facial contour (Fig. 4).

The lower border of the chin should form a smooth continuous line with the lower border of the mandible, and the shape of the chin should enhance the general shape of the face. Females have smaller and more oval shaped chins, whereas males have larger and squarer shaped chins. Dolichoprosopic faces (short and square) are often associated with vertical maxillary deficiency, masseter hyperplasia, wide gonial angles, macrogenia, and Class II deep-bite malocclusions, whereas leptoprosopic faces (long, oval, and narrow) are often associated with vertical maxillary excess, a narrow nose, mandibular anteroposterior deficiency, narrow gonial angles, microgenia, a high palatal vault, and an anterior open bite.

Figure 4. The relationship of the height of the face (Tr-Me) to the width (Za-Za) should be 1.3:1 for females and 1.35 for males. The bigonial (Go-Go) width should be approximately 30% less than the bizygomatic (Za- Za) width.

Transverse Facial Dimensions

The "rule of fifths" is a convenient method to evaluate the transverse proportions of the face. The face is sagittally divided into 5 equal parts, each the approximate width of the eye, from helix of the outer ear (Fig. 2).

Figure 5. Transverse facial proportions and facial form. The "rule of fifths" is a convenient method of evaluating transverse proportions. The intercanthal width should be equal to the alar base width (1), the width of the nasal dorsum should be approximately half the alar base width (2), the width of the medial irides of the eyes should coincide with the corners of the mouth (3), the width and shape of the chin should be in harmony with the rest of the face (4), the Gonion should fall on a line drawn through the outer canthus of the eye (5), and the bigonial width is usually 30% less than the bizygomatic width (6).

Outer Fifths

This is measured from the helix of the ear to the outer corner of the eye and is an indication of the width of the ears. "Bat ears" can be camouflaged by an appropriate hair style. However, otoplastic surgical procedures are relatively atraumatic and can significantly improve the facial appearance.

Medial Two-Fifths

These are measured from the outer to the inner canthi of the eyes. The outer border should coincide with the gonial angles of the mandible. In patients with long and narrow faces, the gonial angles will fall medial to this line, whereas in patients with broad and square faces, the gonial angles will fall lateral to these lines. Within these fifths, it should be noted that the distance between the inner margins of the irides of the eyes should be equal to the width of the mouth. Abnormal interpupillary distance and intercanthal distance are often observed in syndromic patients and can only be altered with craniofacial surgery.

Middle Fifth

This is demarcated by the lines through the inner canthus of the eyes. In patients with hypertelorism, this fifth is relatively larger than the others. The ala of the nose (alar base width) should coincide with these lines, whereas the nasal dorsum should be approximately half of the intercanthal distance. For patients in whom maxillary advancement and/or superior repositioning is planned, this measurement should be considered, and surgical control of the alar base may be indicated.[23].

Applications of the classification of facial types

The classification of facial types has a number of advantages for diagnosis, prognosis, and treatment-planning objectives. It permits one to distinguish skeletal from dental malocclusions. This distinction is a real one because it identifies the degree of severity of the total problem. By definition, a skeletal malocclusion is a dental malocclusion with additional skeletal imbalance. This means that facial esthetics problems are present with skeletal malocclusion. Frequently the degree of severity of the malocclusion is greater when associated with skeletal imbalance. Furthermore, malocclusions associated with skeletal imbalances are more stable than those confined to the dental arches only. Finally, their prognoses with and without treatment are different.

The classification of facial types permits the evaluation of physiologic differences. So far, the first studies on this subject have consisted of the evaluation of muscular activity typically associated with extreme facial types. This indicates differences of forces in the different masticatory muscles.

Facial esthetics

Very few studies have been directly devoted to facial esthetics in a scientific manner that would permit one to distinguish which dimensions of the face and teeth are primarily responsible for a pleasing or unpleasing face.Poulton made an initial attempt which would indicate that large lower face heights associated more with unpleasing faces than anteroposterior variations or a small lower face height. In other words, it seems that (although it is dangerous to generalize) our society frowns upon open-bite facial types, either Class II or Class III, and accepts more easily the deep-bite skeletal type.

Racial frequencies

Comparison between major racial groups would show that the Mongoloid and Negroid races have a greater tendency toward open- bite skeletal types. In other words, a greater frequency of open-bite skeletal type is present in these racial groups. This may be an indication that classifications of facial type, although applicable to many racial groups, should be modified for each race if they have to be defined in precise terms. It may also indicate that facial types are genetically established.

Heredity

Family-line studies did show that when both parents had open- bite skeletal facial types there was a very strong tendency for the offspring to have an open-bite skeletal facial type.

Growth

Sassouni and Nanda have shown that in the open-bite skeletal type mandibular growth is predominantly vertical, whereas in deep-bite it is primarily horizontal. These findings were studied again on a longitudinal basis by Sahni who confirmed that the pattern of growth differs relative to facial type[24].

CHAPTER NINE

PROFILE CHANGES IN GROWING FACE

Facial growth is best understood when discussed according to changes in the transverse, anteroposterior, and vertical dimensions. The transverse facial growth dimension is completed first. The midpalatal suture normally fuses during the second decade and is difficult, although not impossible, to modify after that time. The mandibular symphysis is fused at birth or during the first year. These skeletal patterns of both the upper and lower jaw are, therefore, established early, which is one reason that constriction of the palate should be addressed relatively early. Some additional transverse facial growth occurs because of the apposition on the lateral surfaces of the maxilla and on the alveolus (i.e., the portion of the jaws where the teeth are located) with tooth eruption.

With the exception of the maxillary width, the face is growing downward and forward when the body is growing but can continue well into adolescence and adulthood? Significant changes occur in the third and even fourth decades (i.e., 20-40 yrs of age). The maxilla is moving anteroinferiorly relative to the anterior cranial base and is accompanied by appositional changes at the maxillary tuberosities and along the oral palatal surface. This change makes space for the eventual eruption of the maxillary molars. Simultaneously, the anterior surface of the maxilla and nasal surfaces of the palate are resorptive.

The nasal septum moves in synchrony with the maxilla and may provide some guidance of growth and mechanical support. The mandible also has appositional and resorptive changes that are in concert with endochondral condylar growth. The changes seem to be a response to functional demands on the mandible. Small changes in the chin area are accompanied by minimum apposition on the lateral aspects of the mandibular body. Considerable apposition occurs on the posterior surfaces of the ramus. Concurrently, resorption on the inner surface of the mandibular body and the anterior surface of the ramus occurs, a process that makes little change in the size of the anterior mandible but certainly makes space for the erupting molars as it lengthens the mandibular body.

Adults, children, and adolescents are dynamic and maintain the growth potential for changes of the craniofacial features. Although growth of the adult skeleton is of considerable duration, the small increments make therapeutic changes by current techniques impractical. Unfortunately, post treatment changes produced by this growth can disrupt previously established relationships.

Boys seem more likely to have significant late adolescent and early adult lower jaw growth that results in forward positioning of the lower jaw than are girls, these changes, combined with the average forward mandibular rotation in boys, produce considerable flattening of the profile. For girls, profile flattening is less dramatic because, although all the changes in the soft tissue are similar, they are of less magnitude than are those in boys, and the average backward mandibular rotation mitigates the flattening. Facial profiles tend to be judged as more attractive when the circumoral area is more prominent- a tendency that runs counter to these normal maturation changes.[25]

Profile Changes from 5 to 45 Years of Age

Bishara et al. in a longitudinal study concluded that the timing of the greatest changes in the soft tissue profile occurs earlier in females (10 to 15 years) than in males (15 to 25 years) and the angle of soft tissue convexity that excludes the nose expresses little change between 5 and 45 years. Of the subjects evaluated between 5 and 25 years of age, 17 demonstrated a decrease in convexity, 8 demonstrated no change, and 10 demonstrated an increase in facial convexity with growth. There was an average decrease in facial convexity between 25 and 45 years of age.

The upper and lower lips became significantly more retruded in relation to the esthetic line between 15 and 25 years of age in both males and females and similar trends continued between 25 and 45 years of age.

Bishara et al. longitudinally evaluated untreated normal individuals (15 males and 15 females) at ages 25 and 46. The male skeletal profile tended to increase in convexity because of an increase in the prominence of the maxilla, whereas the female skeletal profile tended to increase in convexity because of a posterior rotation of the mandible.Formby et al. concluded that females showed more changes in soft and hard tissue measurements after 25 years of age than before, whereas most hard tissue changes in males had been accomplished by the age of 25 but not soft tissue changes.[26]

Very few studies have been dedicated to the analysis of soft tissues. Subtelny s studied the soft tissue changes by comparing tracings of serial cephalometric roentgenograms, and in so doing, demonstrated some general principles and trends of soft tissue growth. The growth of the nose seems to be related to the skeletal growth to a certain extent, but the soft tissue growth is probably mostly responsible for the differences in size between boys and girls. Girls show a decline in nasal growth, whereas boys show an increase in growth velocity after the age of 12 years. At 9 years of age, girls grow very quickly, whereas boys are still growing slowly; at their preadolescent rate.

The age at which the growth rate is the same for boys and girls is determined by the intersection of the velocity curves for boys and girls, usually around the age of 12. The nasolabial angle is larger in girls than in boys and decreases with age more in girls than in boys. The reason for this may be that the tip of the nose is sustained by the nasal septum and the ANS. The ANS is carried forward with age. The A point is moving relatively distally with age, and the upper lip is growing only slightly in the vertical direction, especially in girls. The upper lip length showed hardly any increase in the age span studied. In girls, the growth velocity decreased during puberty.

Talass et al. also showed in their study that the length of the upper lip remains almost unchanged. The distance between the tip of the incisor and the lowest point of the upper lip, is larger in girls than in boys and increases more in girls than in boys, indicating that girls will have a higher lip line than boys. The distance from the tip of the incisor to the ANS increases with age in both girls and boys as could be expected with the eruption of the incisor. Since the growth velocity of the upper face height decreases very early in girls, the increase in total face height may be attributed mainly to the growth of the lower jaw and the alveolar processes in girls after puberty.

Vig and Cohen studied vertical growth of the lips in 50 subjects. No attempt was made to control for sex differences, but possible sources of errors were classified. In their study, special attention was paid to avoid variation in radiographic technique and measurement errors, but the extent to which unconscious posture of the lips might have influenced the results is unknown. Further, it should be mentioned that several of the past studies of soft tissue changes are related to orthodontic treatment changes. These studies are not very well suited for comparison with the present data. The present study also shows that the girls with a high gumline should be treated cautiously with intrusion because no spontaneous correction can be expected with age, whereas this may be the case in boys.

The early (before puberty) decrease in the growth velocity of the upper anterior face height in girls should also be taken into account when dealing with patients having problems in the vertical dimension. The upper lip thickness increases with age but the growth velocity decreases during puberty in girls. The lip thickness measured between the subnasale and ANS does not follow this trend exactly because the distance is larger in girls than in boys during puberty.

The lip thickness is larger in boys than in girls because point A apparently moves relatively distally. When interpreting the contour plots, one should bear in mind that the outcome is related to the point of superimpositioning. Yet this very clearly helps to understand growth changes. Regarding the upper lip, sexual dimorphism was demonstrated in the vertical dimension. Furthermore, the position of the upper lip is higher in girls than in boys, in relation to the upper incisor. Regarding the lower lip, the differences related to gender were mostly found in the horizontal direction. Girls stop growing earlier than boys.

The lower lip in boys pouts more than in girls. This cannot be explained by a larger lip thickness (less than 1 mm in boys), but is probably due to a change in lower lip structure. An understanding of the changes in soft tissue during growth is important for the orthodontist. The facial prolife responds to changes in the lips and it may be a key to prediction of stability after orthodontic treatment.[27]

CHAPTER TEN

GROWTH CHANGES IN SOFT TISSUE PROFILE

Successful evaluation of facial balance and harmony includes a study of the facial profile. The relationships of nose, lips and chi are important considerations[28]. Dental and orthodontic interest has long been centered on the developing occlusion and the supporting skeletal structures. The eruption pattern of teeth and the skeletal changes in the cranial and facial areas resulting from progressive growth and development have been studied.[29]

Riedel has stressed that the soft-tissue profile is closely related to the skeletal and dental structures. Subtelny indicated that not all parts of the soft-tissue profile directly follow the underlying skeletal profile. Burstone has suggested that a direct relationship may not always exist because of the variation in the thickness of the soft tissue covering the skeletal face. Stoner and associates concluded that the recontouring of the lips seemed to occur because of the gross movement of the incisor teeth. Neger stated that a proportionate change or improvement in the soft-tissue profile does not necessarily accompany extensive dentition changes.[30]

Facial harmony and balance are determined by the facial skeleton and its soft tissue drape. The architecture and topographic relationships of the facial skeleton form a "foundation" on which the esthetics of the face are based. However, it is the structure of the overlying soft tissues and their relative proportions that provide the visual impact of the face. Soft tissue changes because of growth, as well as mechanotherapy, further add to its importance in orthodontic evaluations.[31]

The growth and development of the dentofacial complex represents a composite of skeletal and integumental changes. However, the facial soft tissues are considered a dynamic structure that can develop along with or independent of their skeletal substructure. Furthermore, their variations in thickness, length, and tonicity may have an effect on the position and relationship of the facial structures.[32]

In the 1930's growth studies of the human head were revolutionized by the introduction of the roentgen cephalometric technique. Since then the skeletal growth of the human profile has been studied by numerous workers. Only a few have studied the growth of the integumental profile, as the general opinion has been that the soft tissue passively reflects the position and form of the underlying skeletal structures. To some extent this might be true, but the studies of Burstone (1959) and Subtelny (1959) have shown that this is only part of the truth, and that soft tissue, within limits, has its own growth potential.[33]

Components of Soft Tissue Profile

Nose

The soft tissue nose is short, rounded, and pug-like. The nasal bridge is low, the nasal profile is concave and the nares can be seen in a face on view. It protrudes very little and is vertically quite short. The human nose continues to grow in a downward and forward direction at least until early adulthood. There does not seem to be an appreciable decrease in the rate of nasal growth which is typical for the skeletal structures. Average yearly increase of 1–1.3mm in the overall length of the external nose is almost the same for males and females.

Nasal Growth and Its Contribution to Profile

In a longitudinal study, Behrents concluded that the upper dorsum rotates upwards and forwards (counter clockwise) approximately 10° between 6 and 14 years of age. The lower dorsum shows both downward and backward (clockwise) and upward and forward (counter clockwise) rotation. This clearly indicated that changes in the nasal dorsum are most closely related to angulation changes of the lower dorsum, particularly during adolescence. The lower dorsum rotates downwards and backwards in persons who show greater vertical and less horizontal growth changes. Rotational changes of the lower dorsum are most closely related with vertical changes at pronasale.

Chaconas showed that Class I subjects have more forward growth of the nasal tip than Class II subjects, Class II subjects tend to have a pronounced elevation of the dorsum and Class III subjects tend to have a concave dorsum.

Subtelny first documented the downward and forward growth of the nose with maturity. The vertical dimension of the nose experiences more growth than the anteroposterior projection in both males and females. There was a spurt seen in male's nasal growth from 10 to 16 years with a peak around 13-14 years. Class II patients exhibited a more pronounced elevation of the bridge of the nose than Class I. Class I cases tended to have straighter noses. Females did not show such a spurt in growth like males but had a more steady increase in nose growth. This is of importance because an orthodontist treating a Class II girl aged 12yrs could expect only minimal increases in nasal projection over the next few years.

However, in a male of a similar age any treatment that causes upper lip retraction in combination with several mm of nose growth might produce a less than optimal final relationship between the lips and nose. When the nose is included in the profile appraisal, the soft tissue profile is seen to be increasing in convexity with progressive growth. This happens because the nose grows in a forward direction to a proportionately greater degree than the other soft tissues of the facial profile.

Wisth stated that as the inclination of the nose remains constant, the profile changes must be due to increments in nose length. This growth is almost linear about 1 millimetre each year. The growth in depth is only half this amount and as it does not change the inclination of the nose, it only seems to compensate the anterior movement caused by the downward growth along the original growth axis, determined by the inclination. This growth will change the position of the tip of the nose in relation to the chin and thus change the profile convexity. In the later stages of development, the nose usually becomes more inclined in a forward direction and the tip of the nose becomes more acute. Vertical dimension of the nose increases until 18years of age.

The upper nose height is found to increase 3 times more than the lower nose height, there by maintaining a ratio of upper nose height to lower nose height of 3:1. The skeletal facial convexity decreases in both sexes, while the soft tissue facial convexity, excluding the nose, is almost unchanged. The total facial convexity, including the nose, increases during the whole period. The result is that even if the skeletal angle indicates a straightening of the face, and the soft tissue angle shows no alterations, the profile, including the nose, shows a definite increase of the convexity. Thus, it seems that the growth of the nose is responsible for most of the profile changes. On the other hand, in an individual with inherently small nose, it may be desirable to institute procedures which will cause the lips to retract. Retraction of the lips and continued facial growth may dramatically improve facial appearance.

Lips

Changes in Lip Length and Thickness Associated with Growth.

Both upper and lower lips grow more than the skeletal lower face in children. In both absolute and proportional terms, the lower lip grows more than the upper lip. Lips grow earlier in girls than boys and in soft tissues as in the skeleton, a cephalocaudal gradient of growth is observed. The upper lip shows rapid increase in length from age1to 3yrs.The rate of growth then reduces from age 3 to 6 yrs when again an upswing occurs till the age of 15yrs. The growth curve for the upper lip is similar to the growth curve for the general body growth curve.

Most children with lip incompetence at age 6 experience self-correction by the age of 16. Lip competence is important in terms of not only esthetics but also stability of overjet correction. In this age group 6–8, it looks as though the incompetency is due to short lips where as it is just incomplete soft tissue growth.Genecov et al. showed in his study that males between the ages of 7 and 17yrs had a greater increase in lip length than females in the same period. The males experienced little more than 2mm in the vertical growth of the upper lip whereas in females it was less than a mm.Mamandras in his study found that in females vertical lip growth was complete by 14yrs where as in males it levelled off at 18yrs.Mandibular lip length increased till 16yrs in females whereas in males it was not completed at 18yrs.

Lip Thickness during Growth and Maturity.

In Subtelny's study, it was found that the upper lip attained a greater thickness in the vermillion region than over point A. This increase in thickness at the vermillion border was approximately equal to the increase in length of the lip. In both males and females, the upper lip increased in thickness from ages 1 to 14. After the age of 14yrs, the lips continued to become thicker in males but not in females. Similarly, in the lower lip the gain in thickness was greater at vermillion border than at pogonion or point B. Lip thickness increase for males from ages 1 to 18yrs was around 7mm while for females it was around 6mm.

Mamandras in his study of lip thickness found that the female lip thickened till the age of 14yrs after which it remained the same till the age of 18yrs and beyond that it showed thinning. Males attained maximum lip thickness by age of 16yrs, after that they too showed thinning.

Nanda et al. slightly differed from the above findings as he found that lip thickness increased uniformly from age 7 to 18yrs and females attained full lip thickness by age 13yrs with slight thinning starting then. In males, however, the thickness continued till the age of 18yrs.

Clinical Applications

The differential in the two sexes with respect to lip thickness implies that the treatment result of extraction therapy of the facial profile will be more noticeable in female than male patients. Because female lips do not thicken with age, any extraction plan for females with straight to convex profiles should be cautiously considered. Lip fullness in relation to the nose which will continue to grow should also be noted.

Inspite of progressive increase in length, both lips show a fairly constant vertical relationship to their respective alveolar processes. After the full eruption of the central incisors, there is little increase in the vertical distance between the crest of the alveolar process and the vermillion border of the lip. The lips also maintain an equally constant relationship to the incisal edges of the anterior teeth.This is of great clinical importance because surgical over intrusion of maxilla results in an esthetically disastrous aging of the patient's face. The male profile generally was shown to straighten with age with a concomitant retrusion of the lips, whereas the female profile did not straighten nor were the lips retruded.

The A-P posture of the lips is also found to be closely related to their supporting hard tissue structures, that is, the teeth and alveolar processes. The maxillary-mandibular dentitions progressively become more retruded relative to its supporting skeletal bone and to the facial plane of the skeletal profile.

Soft Tissue Chin.

Genecovetal.'s study documented that soft tissue chin thickness in females from age 7 to 9yrs was greater than males. Females only had a 1.6mm increase up to age 18 whereas the males had a 2.4mm increase in soft tissue drape over the chin. As a result both sexes had a similar soft tissue thickness at age 17.

In Nanda's study [29], the soft tissue thickness over the chin, symphysis thickness, and the length of the mandibular corpus, all 3 distances increased with age, the males showing the largest increments. Till 7 years the size of the mandibular corpus was the same for both sexes and the curves progressed parallel to each other till the age of 15 when the male sample had larger increases than the female. Increased chin projection seen in the males was due to the mandibular growth than the increase in soft tissue chin thickness.

Wisth showed that the change of soft tissue thickness on the chin was almost identical to that found over nasion. This meant that soft tissue changes of the chin cannot be responsible for changes in the profile convexity. An old adage is that children with a large symphysis would grow up to have an even larger one. However, when there is little symphysial prominence at the chin, the soft tissue chin can make up the deficiency. The soft tissue structures overlying other skeletal landmarks do not show the same pattern of change as that observed for the bony profile. The average hard tissue profile definitely tends to become straighter with age whereas the analogous soft tissue profile tends to remain comparatively stable in its convexity.

Soft Tissue Profile Changes from 5 to 45 Years of Age.

Bishara et al. in a longitudinal study concluded that the timing of the greatest changes in the soft tissue profile occurs earlier in females (10to15years) than in males(15to25years) and the angle of soft tissue convexity that excludes the nose expresses little change between 5 and 45 years. Of the subjects evaluated between 5 and 25 years of age, 17 demonstrated a decrease in convexity, 8 demonstrated no change, and 10 demonstrated an increase in facial convexity with growth. There was an average decrease in facial convexity between 25 and 45 years of age. The upper and lower lips became significantly more retruded in relation to the esthetic line between 15 and 25 years of age in both males and females and similar trends continued between 25 and 45 years of age.

Bishara et al. longitudinally evaluated untreated normal individuals (15 males and 15 females) at ages 25 and 46. The male skeletal profile tended to increase in convexity because of an increase in the prominence of the maxilla, whereas the female skeletal profile tended to increase in convexity because of a posterior rotation of the mandible.

Formby et al. concluded that females showed more changes in soft and hard tissue measurements after 25 years of age than before, whereas most hard tissue changes in males had been accomplished by the age of 25 but not soft tissue changes.

Nasolabial Angle

With decrease in lip prominence and lowering of the nasal tip, nasolabial angle becomes more acute. As nasal tip descends and rotates, the lip descends with it in what is termed as a clockwise rotation of the nasolabial complex. The nasolabial angle decreases slightly from 7 to 18 years in both sexes. The mean at 7 years was 107.8 ± 9.4 degrees for males and 114.7 ± 9.5 degrees for the females. At 18 years, the mean was slightly reduced to 105.8± 9.0and110.7 ± 10.9 degrees.

Mentolabial Angle

The mentolabial angle decreases slightly from 7 to 18 years in both sexes. The mean at 7 years was 125.3 ± 8.4 degrees for males and 136.1 ± 11.6 degrees for the females. At 18 years, the mean was reduced to 125.1 ± 12.9 and 127.1 ± 12.9 degrees. It would be reasonable to assume that individuals would appear less protrusive as they age, due to a number of factors. The maxillary incisors are continually uprighting during adulthood and with the continued growth of the nose, repositioning of the lips, and the vertical increases, one could easily envision that the adult would appear less protrusive overtime.

The mandible increases in size in both males and females, but in the male the occlusal plane tends to flatten and the gonial angle becomes more acute. The net effect is a tendency for a continued counter clockwise rotation of the mandible. In the female, more vertical change is evident and the mandible appears to be rotating clockwise. The possibility that continued growth differences in males and females might suggest a greater possibility of relapse of female Class II cases than male Class II cases and of male Class III cases than female Class III cases. Conversely, male Class II and female Class III corrections might be enhanced.

Smile Changes with Age

As a person ages, the smile gets narrower vertically and wider transversely. The dynamic measures indicate that the muscles' ability to create a smile decreases with increasing age. A study by Desai et al. showed a decrease of 1.5 to 2mm in maxillary incisor display during smile with increasing age. No subject in the 50 and overage group had a high smile and no subject in the 15-to-19-year group had a low smile. All dynamic measurements indicated a pattern of decreasing change from rest to smile, especially evident after ages 30 to 39 years.

VanderGeld et al. found that, in older subjects, maxillary lip line heights decreased significantly in all situations. Lip line heights during spontaneous smiling were reduced by approximately 2mm. In older participants, the mandibular lip line heights also changed significantly and the teeth were displayed less during spontaneous smiling. Mandibular tooth display in the rest position increased significantly. Upper lip length increased significantly by almost 4mm in older subjects, whereas upper lip elevation did not change significantly. The significant increasing lip coverage of the maxillary teeth indicates that the effects of age should be included in orthodontic treatment planning.

In Males. The general soft tissue changes between the ages of 18-42 included the following finding: the profile straightened, the lips became more retrusive. The nose increased in size in all dimensions. There was increased soft tissue thickness at the pogonion. There was decreased upper lip thickness and slightly increased lower lip thickness.

In Females. The profile did not become straighter and the lips did not become more protrusive. The nose increased in size in all dimensions. There was decreased soft tissue thickness at the pogonion. There was upper lip thickness and slightly increased lower lip thickness. Orthodontic treatment that diminishes lower facial height, reduces lip projection, decreases maxillary incisor display, or deepens the lateral nasal grooves should be avoided if possible because they hasten facial aging characteristics.

Features Associated with Aging

As a person ages, lower part of the face appears to lengthen, the interlabial line descends, and the number of vertical fibers in the upper lip reduces. The philtral columns become less prominent and the vermillion becomes a straightline. Jowling and increased nasolabial folds are seen. The M and W shapes of the lips may become straight and the commissures droop giving the look of a frown. Crow's feet at lateral corners of the eyes, horizontal lines on the forehead, vertical corrugations overlying the glabella, vertical furrows along the upper lip, horizontal crease above the chin, and a "turkey gobbler" bag of skin sagging down the skin below the chin can also be seen.

As general loss of body weight occurs, resorption of subcutaneous adipose tissue results in surplus of skin leading to sagging, wrinkling, and creasing. The distribution of collagenous matrix changes, fibres increase in massiveness, and whole skin decreases in resilience. The fibroblasts decline in number and cellular activities. Thus, there is a decrease of hydrophilic protein mucopolysaccharides leading to shrunken facial volume. There is darkening of skin below eyes because of more visible venous plexus in the thinned suborbital hypodermis. The suborbital integument also begins to sag to form bags. Orthodontic tooth movement as a result of bone modeling and remodeling also depends greatly on age-related changes of the skeleton. Cortical bone becomes denser while the spongeous bone reduces with age and the structure changes from that of a honeycomb to a network.[34]

An understanding of the changes in soft tissue during growth is important for the orthodontist. The facial prolife responds to changes in the lips and it may be a key to prediction of stability after orthodontic treatment.[35]

CHAPTER ELEVEN

ORTHODONTIC RELEVANCE

Clinical orthodontists recognize that most persons who seek orthodontic treatment do so because of a desire for improvement in facial harmony. This includes attaining harmony of the teeth with each other, harmonious relationships among the integumental features of the face, and esthetic proportions between the teeth and the soft-tissue facial structures.

The orthodontist seeks to achieve not only these goals but also functional and physiologic harmony of the dentition. As his knowledge of biomechanics, growth, and computers has increased and as corrective appliances have improved, he has become more capable of bringing about desired corrective changes in the esthetic conformity of a patient's face.

The full responsibility for undesirable facial alterations in a patient is often shouldered by the orthodontist when, in reality, the changes are a product of physiologic development and thus beyond his influence. Conversely, orthodontists may take credit for gratifying results after orthodontic therapy when these same physiologic factors of growth and development have been the more important factors in moulding facial contours.

Many investigators endeavour to show the course of normal development of the skeletal and integumental profiles by longitudinal and serial studies which depict the changes by growth alone. Others are interested in the effects of orthodontic treatment upon the facial profile, exclusive of growth. Of prime importance to the clinician in predicting the changing contour of the face is the cumulative effect of growth, development, and treatment upon the patients who come to his office for treatment. (36)

The question of facial balance and harmony orthodontics has engaged the profession from its earliest beginnings to the present time. Norman Kingsley devoted a special chapter on the balance and harmony of facial contours and their relationship to dental and skeletal structures. He recognized the infinite variety of human countenance and equally infinite diversity in the form of the jaws, but emphasized that the attractiveness of facial features is dependent on harmonious relationships of the dentition and the facial configuration. Edward

H. Angle accepted the face of Apollo Belvedere and the dentition based on the skull of "Old Glory" as ideal standards for the orthodontic profession. A casual glance however, will show that the incisor teeth of "Old Glory" protrude too much to be in harmony with Apollo's facial profile (Fig 1) (37)

Figure1- The profile of Apollo Belvedere and the dentition of "Old Glory."

The concept of facial beauty and harmony has changed over the centuries. Facial beauty can be defined as harmony and balance among facial proportions, established by skeletal structures, teeth, and soft tissue. The desire to improve one's dentofacial esthetics is one of the main reasons patients seek orthodontic treatment. Changes in the soft tissue profile are closely related to dental and skeletal changes, caused by either orthodontic treatment or growth. (38)

Assessment of a Balanced Facial Profile

It is interesting to examine how orthodontic standards of normality and reference values were derived and what they actually represent. Out of more than 35 cephalometric analysis that appeared from 1937 to 1969 in the American orthodontic literature, only one study used a sample that reflected the general public's judgment of beauty.

Reidel in 1957 used 30 beauty contest winners for his sample, while all the other cephalometric analyses used samples characterized by a good occlusion only and/or the author's perception of an average or balanced face. Many orthodontic cephalometric standards therefore represent the author's personal opinion of "good esthetics" or simply the average characteristics of a particular population with good occlusion. This may very well represent the average or normal facial pattern and not necessarily the best or most beautiful in the eyes a given population.The perception of beauty may also be influenced by factors such as culture or society and time. Some studies have shown that American blacks have a stronger preference for white features than do African blacks, which may be the result of living in a majority white society.

Figure 2 shows an African American female whose chief complaint was excessive lip fullness. After maxillary and mandibular segmental osteotomies for maximum retraction, the patient was satisfied with a more Caucasian-like profile. One may argue, however, that the pre-treatment profile was more "exotic."

Figure2. Pre-treatment profile. Patient's complaint was too much lip fullness (A). Post-treatment profile after segmental osteotomies. Lip protrusion was reduced significantly (B).

A recent study, in fact, showed that the African American profile currently presented by models in the mass media is not "Caucasian-like"; in fact, the Caucasian models in the study displayed more black features than African American models did white features. This suggests that concepts of facial beauty may be changing with time. Hier in 1999, for instance, showed that both male and female whites prefer a lip position that is more protrusive than Ricketts E-line standard, defined in 1968. A study conducted at the University of Oklahoma showed that more lip protrusion was acceptable for both male and female profiles when a large nose, or especially when a large chin, was present. It was also found that more lip protrusion was desirable for women than for men. Regardless of the profile preference, the orthodontist must understand the behavior of the soft tissues during growth and its response to different treatment modalities so that individual esthetic preferences can be met, or at least avoid detrimental effects on the facial profile.

Profile Lines for Evaluating the Face

Ricketts defined the esthetic plane (E-plane) as a line tangent to the chin and the tip of the nose. In white adults, the lower lip should lie 4+3 mm behind this plane. The upper lip lies slightly behind the lower lip. In children, the lower lip lies on this plane or slightly behind it as a result of the delayed development of the chin and the nose. In African American and Chinese adults, the lower lip lies 1 to 3 mm ahead of the E-planes (Fig 3)

Fig 3 - Ricketts Esthetic Plane (E-plane)

Gonzales Ulloa suggested dropping a vertical line through soft tissue glabella to evaluate the position of the chin. Soft tissue pogonion should lie close to this line (Fig 4).

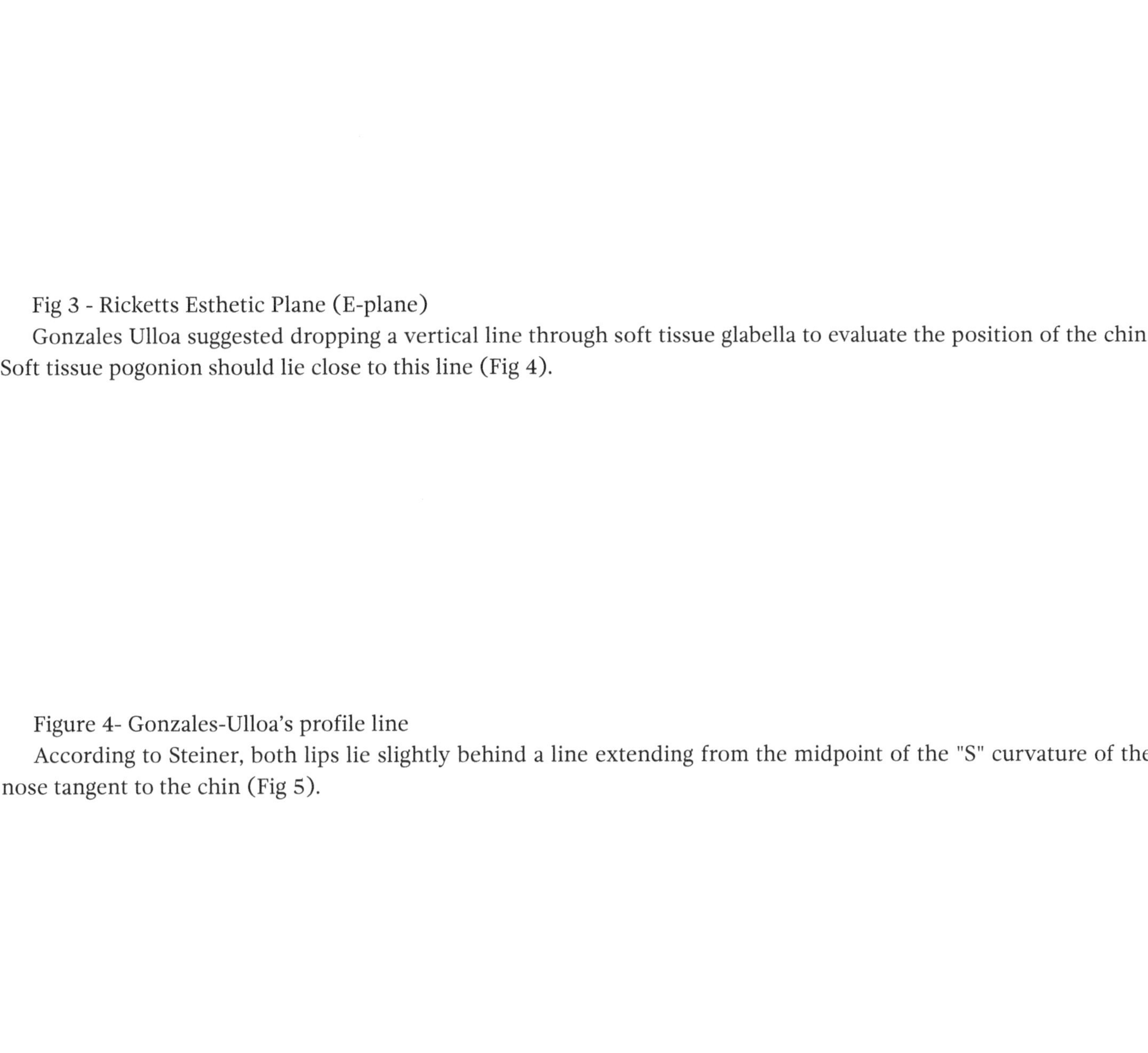

Figure 4- Gonzales-Ulloa's profile line

According to Steiner, both lips lie slightly behind a line extending from the midpoint of the "S" curvature of the nose tangent to the chin (Fig 5).

Figure 5- Steiner's profile line

Merrifield's Z-line is drawn tangent to the chin and the more protruding lip (usually the upper). The lower lip should lie on the line or slightly behind it. In white adults, the line intersects with the horizontal at an angle of 80 °$\pm$ 5 °. In a sample of 11- to 15-year-old children, the Z-angle measured 78 ° +5 ° (Fig 6).

Figure 6. Merrifield's Z-line

Holdaway's profile line extends from the chin through the upper lip and intersects the nose approximately 10 mm behind its tip. If the ANB angle is 2 °, the profile line intersects the NB line at an angle of 8 ° (Fig 7).

Figure 7. Holdaway's profile line.

Bishara et al found that Holdaway's soft tissue angle is an age-dependent measurement and progressively decreases from 5 to 45 years of age. Burstone measured facial convexity as the angle between glabella to subnasale and subnasale to soft tissue pogonion (Fig 8).

Figure 8. Burstone's facial contour angle

In his sample on young adult whites, the facial contour angle was -11.3 °. The upper lip extends 3.5 ± 1.4 mm beyond the line connecting subnasale and soft tissue pogonion, and the lower lip extends 2.2 + 1.6 mm beyond this line (Fig 9).

Figure 9. Burstone's lip protrusion evaluation line

Burstone also defined two important angles, which are the nasolabial angle and the chin throat angle, which are on average 114 ° in males, 118 ° in females, and 114 ° in males, 106 ° in females, respectively (Fig 10)

Figure 10. Nasolabial angle and chin-throat angle.

Soft Tissue Changes with Treatment

Effects of Extraction and Non extraction Therapy

Caplan and Shivapuja studied the effect of four first-premolar extractions on the soft tissue profile of 28 adult female African American patients. They found that individual variation in lip response is great (the upper lip is more variable than the lower lip to differences in incisor retraction). They also found that the nasolabial angle became more obtuse, but the labiomental angle was not significantly affected; the length of the upper and lower lips remained unchanged and the upper and lower lips thickened.

Lo and Hunter showed a correlation of 0.77 between lower anterior face height, measured from the anterior nasal spine to Menton, and the nasolabial angle, inferring that an opening rotation of the mandible during treatment would cause an increase in the nasolabial angle.

Waldman reported an unpredictable change in the nasolabial angle with upper incisor retraction. Talass et al studied the soft tissue response of Class II Division I female patients to orthodontic treatment. To eliminate the effects of growth, they used a sample of untreated controls. They found that changes in the lower lip, in response to orthodontic tooth movement, were more predictable than those of the upper lip.

Rains and Nanda reported that the upper lip response was related to both upper and lower incisor movement, and that there was greater variability of the lower lip than the upper lip to incisor movement. This is contrary to the findings of Talass et al and Caplan and Shivapuja.

Young and Smith examined soft tissue profiles of 198 orthodontic patients treated with full fixed appliances without extraction of any permanent teeth. The sample selection criteria was designed to allow direct comparison with Drobocky and Smith, who examined patients with premolar extractions. They found that on average, non-extraction patients had less facial change as a result of orthodontic treatment--the mean differences between the two groups being 6 ° in the nasolabial angle, 1 to 2 mm in upper lip protrusion, and 2 to 3 mm in lower lip protrusion.

However, the range of individual changes in the facial profile was almost as great for non-extraction cases as for extraction cases. This suggests that individual growth changes and unpredictable treatment response may play a role in the variability of treatment results for the soft tissue profile.

The inability to formulate constant strong correlations between soft and hard tissues indicates that the change in the perioral soft tissues is a complex phenomenon. Some researchers have found factors that may explain this variability.

Oliver stated that lip thickness, postural tone, and body fat may influence the soft tissue's response to incisor retraction. Holdaway described lip taper as the difference in the thickness of the upper lip at a point 3 mm inferior to point A and at the vermilion border. If the difference between these measurements is more than 1 mm, this difference must adjust before lip retraction occurs. Exceptions exist when the tissue near point A is very thick and the lip may not follow the incisors at all, or if the tissue near point A is very thin, the lip may immediately follow the incisor, regardless of lip taper. In adults, even if lip taper is present, the lips will usually follow the teeth immediately, because the lips have accommodated to their position over a long period.

Kokodynski et al found a statistically significant correlation between maxillary incisor and lip retraction in both male and female patients who had thin, highly strained lips. As lip thickness increased and lip strain decreased, correlations became non-significant, making it more difficult to predict upper lip changes resulting from maxillary incisor retraction. A good example of how unpredictable soft tissue response to treatment can be is seen with a pair of monozygotic, male, 10-year-old twins who were treated at the University of Illinois. They both presented with very similar malocclusions and almost identical soft tissue profiles (Fig 11).

Figure 11. Pre-treatment profile (extraction twin) (A). Pre-treatment profile (non-extraction twin) (B). Pre-treatment cranial base superimposition of extraction twin (dashed line) and non-extraction twin (solid line) (C).

One twin was treated with non-extraction and the other twin had extraction of four first bicuspids. After treatment, both twins still presented almost identical skeletal relationships; however, the soft tissue profile was different (Fig 12).

Figure 12. Post-treatment profile (extraction twin) (A). Post-treatment profile (non-extraction twin) (B). Post-treatment cranial base superimposition of extraction twin (dashed line) and non-extraclion twin (solid line) (C).

The upper incisor of the non-extraction twin was protruded 1.5 mm, and the upper lip did not change in relation to the E-line; the lower incisor was proclined 4 mm, and the lower lip came forward 2.5 mm in relation to the E-line. The extraction twin, on the other hand, showed 2 mm of retraction of the upper incisor and 3 mm of retraction of the upper lip in relation to the E-line. There was 1 mm of retraction of the lower incisor and 1 mm of retraction of the lower lip.

This twin also showed an increase in nose projection of 1 mm greater that the non- extraction twin, which may explain why there was more upper lip retraction than actual retraction of the upper incisors. Despite being identical twins, the upper and lower lip response to incisor position change was not uniform in both twins. The upper lip in the non- extraction twin did not change after 1.5 mm of incisor protrusion, and the lower lip protruded at a ratio of 1:1.6 to lower incisor protrusion. In the extraction twin, both the upper and lower lips retracted at a ratio of almost 1:1 to upper and lower incisor retraction, respectively.

Subnasale is the landmark where the upper lip meets the inferior border of the nose and is also referred to as the attachment of the upper lip. This point is relatively unchangeable from the standpoint of treatment; therefore, it is very important to consider because it plays a role in the drape of the upper lip. Robinson, in a study of a young edentulous sample, showed that there is a relaxed lip position that is independent of teeth and the supporting alveolar process; therefore, lip posture must be evaluated from a relaxed lip position. The patients shown in Figures 13 and 14 have a Class II Division 1 malocclusion. The patient in Figure 13 is characterized primarily by a maxillary dental protrusion and lip strain. The patient in Figure 14 has a slight maxillary dental protrusion, a retrognathic mandible, and an obtuse nasolabial angle. The problem with the patient in Figure 13 is very successfully treated by orthodontic means, because the retraction of the upper lip will follow incisor retraction and facial esthetics will improve. The patient in Figure 14, however, is best treated by a surgical procedure to advance the mandible.

Because subnasale cannot be changed, any further retraction of the upper incisors will fail to retract the lip when it is in a relaxed position, but may cause the nasolabial angle to become more obtuse on lip closure, with detriment to facial esthetics.

Figure 13. Class II patient with maxillary dental protrusion and lip strain (A). Post-treatment profile after premolar extractions and retraction of anterior teeth (B). Lip strain was reduced, and good balance and harmony of the lips was obtained.

Figure 14. Class II patient with slight maxillary dental protrusion and retrognathic mandible (A). Post- treatment profile after premolar extraction and retraction of anterior teeth (B). Tile increased nasolabial angle and still retrognathic mandible produces less than ideal facial balance.

Effect of Headgear versus Functional Appliances

Johnston suggested that the major effect of functional appliances for Class II correction is the prevention of maxillary dentoalveolar compensation. When compared with untreated controls, the major long-term difference, therefore, is a midfacial dentoalveolar retrusion in the Class II patients treated with a functional appliance. In the process of producing this relative retrusion, the normal pattern of mandibular growth is allowed to produce the molar and incisal correction.

Tulloch et al found that headgear patients had a greater tendency to restricted maxillary forward movement, while functional appliance subjects had more increased mandibular length and improved chin position. There was such wide variation within the groups, however, that much of the differences may in fact be more attributable to differences in growth and clinician proficiency than to a particular treatment approach. They were unable to identify any patient characteristics that could serve as useful predictors of treatment response.

Pancherz reported short and long term effects of the Herbst appliance on the facial profile. In relation to the E-line, the upper lip became retrusive, while the lower lip remained, on average, unchanged. When excluding the nose, the facial profile convexity was, on average, reduced in the stable group, and it remained unchanged in the relapse group. As a result of post-treatment growth changes, however, the long term effects of therapy on the facial profile were variable and unpredictable.

Unfortunately, there are no studies that show differences in soft tissue response to headgear versus functional appliance treatment. What is known from the study by Tulloch et al is that the functional appliance group had, on average, 3 ° more proclination of the lower incisors than the control or headgear groups.

We can conclude, therefore, that the dentoalveolar compensations that produce the Class II dental corrections vary slightly between these two treatment modalities, because greater lower anchorage loss may be expected with the use of a functional appliance. This phenomenon may be beneficial, for instance, for the Class II patient with a straight or obtuse nasolabial angle and for whom surgical mandibular advancement is not an option.

Maxillary Protraction

Most studies have shown that significant soft tissue profile changes can be expected with maxillary protraction primarily as a result of a decrease in soft tissue facial angle and protrusion of the upper lip area resulting in better lip competence and posture. However, individual variations exist in treatment response and subsequent growth changes.

Ngan et al studied the soft tissue profile changes in 20 patients with skeletal Class III malocclusions treated consecutively with maxillary expansion and protraction headgear. They found that a corresponding forward movement of the soft tissue of 50% to 79% accompanied the forward movement of the maxilla. In the mandible, the downward and backward movement of the soft tissues was equivalent to 71% to 81% of the corresponding soft tissues. (39)

The practical value of knowing the high relationship that exists between the orthodontically affected hard and soft tissues lies in estimating the changes in the perioral soft-tissue profile. This can be accomplished by means of a regression equation with the range established by the standard error of estimate, or it can be done by scatter diagrams.

Establishment of a prediction of the range of soft-tissue change in a specific area, could greatly aid diagnosis and prognosis. There are many areas yet to be fully evaluated and understood in conjunction with these relationships. These include such factors as growth and development, heredity, and environmental conditions.

The effect of large ANB differences, the positional relationship of the upper incisor upon the lower lip, and adipose tissue was under consideration but was not fully analysed. These factors could have some bearing upon the variations found in the predictability of the results. With a better understanding of what to expect or to strive for in treatment, orthodontic thinking may be stimulated with respect to the soft-tissue structures around the mouth and the total esthetic facial problem, thus benefiting both orthodontist and patient. (40)

Aesthetic factors are still the main attraction underlying the reasons for patients to undergo orthodontic treatment. Related to this, the key factor in orthodontic diagnosis and treatment plan is a soft tissue evaluation which of course should include the patient's aesthetic expectations. In soft tissue evaluation, one of the facial characteristics that is usually the benchmark is the facial profile. (41).

Esthetic ideals are continuously evolving in today's age of global media and merging cultures. It has been estimated that 3 out of 4 patients come to orthodontists to improve facial attractiveness. (42)

Defining soft tissue treatment objectives will lead the clinician to a treatment plan and mechano therapy that will maximize the facial esthetic outcome. (43) Evaluating facial profiles and facial balance is a continuous learning process for orthodontists. (44).

Some controversy still exists concerning the interdependence of the skeletal structures and their soft tissue covering. Angle (1907) claimed that if the dentition is arranged according to given standards, the soft tissue will shape in a harmonious manner. Riedel (1957) pointed out that the soft tissue profile is closely related to the skeletal and dental structures, whereas Subtelny (1959) stated that the orthodontist cannot assume that the skeletal profile is similar to the soft tissue profile. Burstone (1958) and Neger (1959) also doubted the existence of such an absolute relationship and explained it by the variation in the thickness of the soft tissue draping of the face. The interrelationship between growth, orthodontic treatment and hard and soft tissue profile changes has been described by numerous authors (Subtelny, 1959; Rudee, 1964; Wisth, 1971,1974; Hershey, 1972; Anderson et al., 1973; Angelle, 1973; Koch et al., 1979; Lamastra, 1981; Forsberg and Odenrick, 1981). There is general agreement that orthodontic treatment may influence the soft tissue profile, but there is still disagreement on the amount of response of the soft tissues to changes in the position of the teeth and alveolar process.

Some workers report a definite correlation between incisor movement and soft tissue changes (Stoner et al., 1956; Riedel, 1957; Bloom, 1961; Rudee, 1964; Anderson et al., 1973; Garner, 1974; Roos, 1977; Koch et al., 1979; Oliver, 1982). Others have found that proportional changes in the soft tissue do not follow changes in the dentition (Burstone, 1958; Neger, 1959; Subtelny, 1961; Hershey, 1972; Angelle, 1973; Wisth, 1974). Some authors find that these differences may be attributed to sex (Huggins and McBride, 1975), variation in lip morphology (Oliver, 1982; Holdaway, 1983), amount of incisor retraction (Wisth, 1974), different treatment mechanics (Forsberg and

Odenrick, 1981) or to extraction or non- extraction as part of the treatment (Stromboni, 1979). (45).

CHAPTER TWELVE

CURRENT CONCEPTS

As noted by Pessa, "there are many arbitrary definitions of what constitutes a youthful face but the appearance of youth is not arbitrary; it is simply difficult to define" (Pessa et al., 2008). Facial morphology from infancy to old age is a complex, three-dimensional (3D) interplay of multiple structural tissue layers, and our understanding of this process is in a constant state of evolution and refinement. Current understanding of the facial aging process has historically been largely empirical, given that it has traditionally been based on the effectiveness of various treatments, both surgical and nonsurgical, aimed at rejuvenation but sometimes result in an odd or "done" appearance.[46]Anthropometric statistics derived from geometric models of human faces assist us to understand the diversity of aging and facial perceptions.[47]

The features of a human face, facial components, as well as the human face taken as a whole, act as a biometric tool for purposes of individual human identification. With the advancements in technology and with the introduction of biometric systems for the purpose of identification, automated face recognition (FR) systems have been created to match individual faces from print and digital photographs and video to the faces of an individual with the reference image in a computer database or with the photograph of the suspect.

One of the main problems which is addressed with the facial recognition systems is the change occurring in the face with time or with aging. As the personal identity credentials such as passports, driving licenses and ration cards are valid for years. The primary problem that arises with automated facial recognition systems is to match the two photographs of the same individual from different age groups.

Several researchers have highlighted this temporal performance degradation. To meet this challenge, the approach which needs to be followed is to research the adult age-related craniofacial morphological changes to better understand the process of aging individuals from a facial image, or rather, develop workable artificial age progression techniques to anticipate how an individual's face may appear after several years have passed. The appearance of a human face is affected considerably by aging as shown in a diagrammatical representation in Fig. 1.

Figure 1 Typical aging skin changes.

Albert et al. and Rhodes have reported that facial aging is mainly attributed to bone movement and growth, and skin related deformations associated with the introduction of wrinkles and the reduction of muscle strength. Usually bone growth takes place during childhood whereas during adulthood the most intense age-related deformations are linked with texture changes.

The observation of aging-related features on faces allows humans to estimate the age of other persons just by looking at their face. However, researchers studying the process of age estimation by humans have concluded that humans are not so accurate in age estimation and hence the possibility of developing automatic facial age estimation methods poses an attractive area of research. As adults age, myriad changes occur diachronically within the craniofacial complex. Notable soft tissue modifications can be seen across each decade of adult life that passes. Subtle hard tissue or bony changes slightly alter the overall shape of the human face, mainly in the dentoalveolar region.

These age-related changes affect the accuracy and efficacy of biometric techniques concerning automated facial recognition. A lot of researchers worldwide are working on a wide variety of aspects related to face aging, facial age progression or synthetic facial aging, and facial expression, with the goal of improving computer automated face recognition systems.[48]

Anthropometry

Anthropometry is an art and science used extensively for measuring the soft tissue proportions.

Anthropometric Measurements

Direct anthropometric measurements are made keeping the head position parallel to the ground using magnetic level finder. Subjects were asked to sit in an upright relaxed position and made to look at a distant object. Measurements are performed according to classical methods of physical anthropology using standard instruments (Figs. 2, 3) described by Farkas L. G. Facial proportions are determined, which are clinically significant (Figs. 4, 5).

Fig. 2- Standard instruments used for measuring width of the mouth, lip, length of the nose and naso-labial angle

• 64 •

Fig. 3- Standard instruments used for measuring height of the face, width of the head and mandibular arc

Fig. 4- Sample measurement of width of the mouth

Fig. 5- Sample measurement of height of the face

Various anthropometric landmarks

1. **Eurion (eu)**: most prominent lateral point on each side of the skull in the area of the parietal and temporal bones.
2. **Zygion (zy)**: most lateral point of the zygomatic arch and is identified by trial measurement, not by anatomical relationship. It is identical to the bony zygion of the malar bones.
3. **Gonion (go)**: most lateral point on the mandibular angle close to the bony gonion. It is identified by palpation. If the angle is flat or if there is rich soft tissue cover, determination of this point is very difficult.
4. **Endocanthion (en)**: point at the inner commissure of the eye fissure. This soft endocanthion is located lateral to the bony landmark that is used in cephalometry.
5. **Exocanthion (ex)**: point at the outer cornmissure of the eye fissure. The soft exocantion is slightly medial to the bony exocanthion.
6. **Alare (al)**: most lateral point on each alar contour.
7. **chelion (ch)**: point located at each labial commissure.
8. **Tragion (t)**: notch on the upper margin of the tragus.
9. **Stomion (sto)**: imaginary point at the crossing of the vertical facial midline and horizontal labial fissure between gently closed lips, with teeth shut in the natural position.
10. **Nasion (n)**: point in the midline of the nasal root and the nasofrontal suture. The slight ridge on which it is situated is felt by the observer's fingernail. This point is always above the line that connects the inner canthi. The soft nasion and the bony nasion are identical.
11. **Subnasale (sn)**: midpoint of the columella base at the apex of the angle where the lower border of the nasal septum and the upper lip meet. This point is not identical to the bony subnasion, or nasospinale (ns), which is the midpoint of the anterior margin of the apertura pyriformis at the base of the spina nasalis anterior.

12. **Gnathion (gn):** lowest median landmark on the lower border of the mandible which is identified by palpation and is identical to the bony gnathion.
13. **Labiale superius (Is):** midpoint of upper vermilion line.
14. **Labiale inferius (li):** midpoint of lower vermilion line.

Anthropometry is an art and science used extensively for measuring the soft tissue proportions. While it is true that error is found in measurements of this kind, a great many trends of growth & development and therapy changes can be recorded with a significant degree of accuracy.

It has been shown that the reproducibility of rating of facial aesthetics is good and also opinions between panels were almost similar. Facial proportion varies among the different ethnic groups and today, most of the available studies are done on western population. Hence an anthropometric study can be conducted in the local population.[49]

Leslie G. Farkas (a plastic and reconstructive surgeon) can be said to be the modern father of soft-tissue facial anthropometry publishing. Having published more than 120 scientific articles, he has defined almost every single imaginable facial measurement and index ratio on the human face and is the most highly cited author in the field. He has found a role for anthropometry in evaluation and surgical treatment of numerous congenital craniofacial disorders, including lateral facial dysplasia and cleft palate and in general facial plastic and cosmetic surgery, and has performed work revising the neoclassical canons and studying facial aesthetics numerically.

Computer Programs

Victor Johnston (an evolutionary psychologist) has also recently developed a computer program called Face Prints that uses a genetic algorithm to evolve faces and is attempting to turn it into a useful computer planning system for facial surgery. A similar genetic algorithm has been used to evolve faces from principal components by Hancock.[50]

Photogrammetry

It is a relatively simple method for clinical application and is also relatively non- invasive and low cost. In addition, it avoids inconvenience to the participants and also saves valuable time. Fig- 5

Figure-5: Photographic Technique

The photogrammetric parameters

1. Total facial angle or facial convexity including the nose (N-Prn-Pg) - angle between nasion (N) to tip/pronasale (Prn) line and pronasale (Prn) to pogonion (Pg) line

2. Facial angle or facial convexity excluding the nose (G-Sn-Pg) - angle between glabella to subnasale (Sn) line and subnasale (Sn) to pogonion (Pg) line

3. Nasomentalangle (N-Prn/N-Pg) - angle between nasion (N) to pogonion line (Pg) and nasion to tip (Prn) line

4. Nose tip angle (N-Prn-Cm) - angle between nasion (N) to tip/pronasale line (Prn) and tip to columella (Cm) line

5. Nasolabial angle (Cm-Sn-Ls) - angle between columellar point (Cm) to subnasale line (Sn) and subnasale to labiale superior (Ls) line

6. Mentolabial angle (Li-Sm-Pg) - angle between labiale inferior point (Li) to supramentale line (Sm) and supramentale to pogonion (Pg) line

7. Nasofrontal angle (G-N-Nd) - angle between glabella (G) to nasion (N) line and nasion to nasal dorsum (Nd) line

8. Projection of upper lip to chin (N-Pg/N-Ls) - angle between nasion (N) to pogonion (Pg) line and nasion to labiale superior (Ls) line

9. Upper lip angle (Sn-Ls/Sn-Pg) - angle between subnasale (Sn) to labiale superior (Ls) line and subnasale to pogonion (Pg) line

10. Projection of lower lip to chin (N-Pg/N-Li) - Anglebetween nasion (N) to pogonion (Pg) line and nasion to labiale inferior (Li) line.

Glabella (G), nasion (N), nasal dorsum (Nd), pronasale (Prn), columella (Cm), subnasale (Sn), labiale superior (Ls), labiale inferior (Li), supramentale (Sm), pogonion (Pg)

Angular measurements: nasomental angle (N – Prn/N – Pg); nose tip angle (N – Prn – Cm); nasolabial angle (Cm – Sn – Ls); mentolabial angle(Li – Sm – Pg)

Angular parameters of the nasofrontal angle (G – N – Nd); total facial angle or facial convexity including the nose (N – Prn – Pg); facialangle or angle of facial convexity excluding the nose (G – Sn – Pg)

Projection of the upper lip to chin (N – Pg/N – Ls); upper lip angle (Sn – Ls/Sn – Pg); projection of the lower lip to chin (N – Pg/N – Li)

Photogrammetric analysis has advantages in facial profile analysis on angular measurements, as they are not affected by photographic enlargement.[51]

3D Imaging Systems

From the past to the present, photography and cephalometric radiographs have been used to evaluate facial soft tissue. However, these methods have still some deficiencies. Some variables such as the distance between the subject and the camera, the camera angle, position of the head and settings of the camera may impact the assessments in the evaluation with photos. Also, cephalometric radiographs have some disadvantages such as superimposition, distortion, magnification, errors in patient positioning, and radiation exposure. More importantly, when evaluations were carried out by cephalometric radiographs, three- dimensional (3D) human face would be reduced to two-dimensions (2D), and depth is lost. Because of all these negative situations, 2D imaging systems began to give way to the 3D system. 3D imaging systems are effective, fast, and non-invasive methods that require minimal patient cooperation.

3D imaging systems are used to determine the norms of facial soft tissue in populations, monitor growth and development, evaluate treatment outcomes, and perform soft tissue simulations. Records obtained by non-invasive and non-ionized 3D imaging systems can be repeated in the desired period.

With these advantages, 3D imaging systems are particularly preferred in growth and development studies. While the assessments performed by the 2D system are made along horizontal and vertical directions, 3D images can be carried out along the x (horizontal size), y (vertical dimension), and z (anteroposterior dimension and depth) axes.

In the assessment with 2D imaging system, measurements calculated bird's-eye distance between the 2 shortest coordinates. In 3D imaging systems, the distance between two points can be measured either with bird'seye or surface topography. In addition, angular, proportional, and volumetric measurements can be made, while we can create hundreds of colorful facial maps and image simulations.

Laser Scanning

Laser scanning 3D imaging technology is used for facial soft tissue imaging. The image is taken at 0.5-mm sensitivity and for 8–10 seconds. The length of time obtaining images may cause stabilization distress and loss of the image clarity, especially in infants and young patients.34 Patients close their eyes while the image is taken, so the stabilization of landmarks can be disrupted, in particular around the eyes. A flash in the background may occur in surfaces without soft tissue, and some difficulties may be encountered in identifying landmarks depending on the surface color. Even white light laser applications may lead to some deficiencies for capturing accurate color in the tissue surface.

Stereophotogrammetry

Stereophotogrammetry is an imaging system that transforms the 2-dimensional images obtained by 2 synchronized camera device to the 3D images with the help of computers, and makes processed the complex algorithms process. The system consists of two synchronized cameras angled at 150° and mounted in a frame 50 cm from within. Time of the image capture is up to 1.5 milliseconds, and the processing time is approximately 30 seconds.

The short image capture time especially causes a great advantage for the patient and the physician. High image quality and non-invasive and ionized nature of imaging are advantages. It is a more rapid method according to the laser scanning system, and there are no safety concerns with the laser scanning system in this system.

3Dmd Imaging Systems

Recently, especially in the dental clinic, 3dmd (3Dmd, Atlanta, Ga, USA) face system, which is a stereophotogrammety system, has been started to be used frequently. 3dmd is a surface imaging system and designed to display a 3D human face. The system provides exact size image with face morphology and linear, angular, and volumetric measurements of the human face. Advanced photography speed with high resolution eliminates image distortion caused by patient movement.[52]

The appearance of a human face is affected with aging. Facial aging effects are mainly attributed to bone movement, growth and skin related deformations associated with the introduction of wrinkles and reduction of fat and muscle strength. Usually bone growth takes place during childhood whereas during adult ages the most intense age-related deformations are linked with texture changes. The observation of aging-related features on the face allows humans to estimate the approximate age of other persons which may be accurate. Humans are not so accurate in age estimation hence the possibility of developing automatic facial age estimation methods poses an attractive direction. Human aging is an important aspect of biometrics and also for all face processing applications and has not been studied in depth yet and needs to be explored in different populations further.[53]

Modern society has placed a strong emphasis on physical attractiveness; facial esthetics is an important attribute upon which opinions and perceptions of character ability are conceived. Researchers in cognitive science have proposed that human perception of facial attractiveness could be a biological impetus for mate selection in human reproduction[54]. Orthodontics and other fields of dentistry should follow technological advances strictly in order to use in practice.[55]

CHAPTER THIRTEEN

CONCLUSION

Child face is not a miniature form of adult face. As growth process takes place, the changes in the hard and soft tissues of the face bring about a significant change in structure and profile of the face.[56] Facial esthetics is one of the main goals of orthodontic treatment, and increased emphasis has been placed on it in recent years by both patients and orthodontists.

Traditional orthodontic treatment planning uses profile outlines to assess facial attractiveness. In the same spirit, studies of facial esthetics in orthodontic literature have concentrated on the profile aspect of the face, especially on the profile outline as traced from photographs or cephalometric radiographs. However, attractiveness is the end result of many different factors, many of which are not related to the profile, such as hairstyle, the color and shape of the eyes, the color and texture of the complexion, and the shape of the lateral parts of the face.[57]

In dental practice it is often necessary to assess the skeletal pattern of a patient clinically without the aid of a lateral skull radiograph. The assumption is often made that the soft tissue profile of the patient is a guide to the skeletal pattern; and soft tissue points A and B indicate the relationship of skeletal points A (subspinale) and B (supramentale).[58]

Successful orthodontic treatment is not only to establish a balanced, stable and beautiful occlusal relationship, but also to achieve coordinated soft tissue profile and appearance. In orthodontic treatment, changing the occlusal state of the patient is the first goal pursued by each orthodontist, and for the patient, it seems more attention to the change in facial profile.[59]

Historically, orthodontics has included facial harmony as one of its important goals to accomplish along with occlusal excellence. Angle suggested that if the teeth were placed in optimal occlusion, good facial harmony would result. In more recent years, a large number of researches demonstrated that soft tissues, which vary considerably in thickness between individuals and from one ethnic group to another, are a major factor in determining the final facial profile of the patient.

Nevertheless, various dentoskeletal standards used as goal for treatment ignore soft-tissue thickness in treatment planning. Holdaway and Legan and Burstone developed soft tissue analyses that gained wide acceptance in clinical and research work in both orthodontics and orthognathic surgery. When formulating a treatment plan for the patient, careful consideration should be given to facial contour angle, upper and lower lip protrusion, nasolabial angle, mentolabial sulcus depth and lower face, throat angle.[60]

In the past, treatment has been planned on a basis of norms for occlusion and bony relation!. More attention should be paid to soft tissues and the psychological implications to the individual patients. The method described has its imperfections, but it allows measurement of all the soft tissues of the face, which include the eyes, the nose and the mouth. It should therefore allow consideration to be given to those aspects of facial morphology of particular concern to the patient and the chances of improvement. Sophisticated computer graphics are able to present 'reconstituted' faces but are expensive and are not included in the modest computer graphic system described here, which is intended for the individual clinician in oral surgery or orthodontics who wishes to analyse his results insofar as they affect the soft tissues of the face.[61]

Knowledge about the age changes of jaws and soft tissue profile will help the dentists to aid in decision making to arrive at a comprehensive treatment plan and achieve better treatment efficiency.[62]

CHAPTER FOURTEEN

BIBLIOGRAPHY

1. Sharma P, Arora A, Valiathan A. Age changes of jaws and soft tissue profile. The Scientific World Journal. 2014;2014.

1. Prahl-Andersen B, Ligthelm-Bakker AS, Wattel E, Nanda R. Adolescent growth changes in soft tissue profile. American Journal of Orthodontics and Dentofacial Orthopedics. 1995 May 1;107(5):476-83.

3. Bishara SE, Jakobsen JR, Hession TJ, Treder JE. Soft tissue profile changes from 5 to 45 years of age. American Journal of Orthodontics and Dentofacial Orthopedics. 1998 Dec 1;114(6):698-706.

4. Almurtadha RH, Alhammadi MS, Fayed MM, Abou-El-Ezz A, Halboub E. Changes in soft tissue profile after orthodontic treatment with and without extraction: A systematic review and meta-analysis. Journal of Evidence Based Dental Practice. 2018 Sep 1;18(3):193-202.

5. Bolla SC, Gantha NS, Sheik RB. Review of history in the development of esthetics in dentistry. J Dent Med Sci. 2014;13(6):31-5.

6. Peck S, Peck L. Selected aspects of the art and science of facial esthetics. In Seminars in orthodontics 1995 Jun 1 (Vol. 1, No. 2, pp. 105-126). WB Saunders.

7. Sarvera DM, Ackermanb JL. Orthodontics about face: the re-emergence of the esthetic paradigm. American Journal of Orthodontics and Dentofacial Orthopedics. 2000 May 1;117(5):575-6.

8. Heppt WJ, Vent J. The facial profile in the context of facial aesthetics. Facial Plastic Surgery. 2015 Oct;31(05):421-30.

9. Sharma P, Arora A, Valiathan A. Age changes of jaws and soft tissue profile. The Scientific World Journal. 2014;2014

10. Dimaggio FR, Ciusa V, Sforza C, Ferrario VF. Photographic soft-tissue profile analysis in children at 6 years of age. American Journal of Orthodontics and Dentofacial Orthopedics. 2007 Oct 1;132(4):475-80.

11. Sharma P, Arora A, Valiathan A. Age changes of jaws and soft tissue profile. The Scientific World Journal. 2014;2014.

12. Sveikata K, Balciuniene I, Tutkuviene J. Factors influencing face aging. Literature review. Stomatologija. 2011;13(4):113-6.

13. Mendelson B, Wong CH. Changes in the facial skeleton with aging: implications and clinical applications in facial rejuvenation. Aesthetic plastic surgery. 2012 Aug 1;36(4):753-60.

14. Soh J, Chew MT, Wong HB. A comparative assessment of the perception of Chinese facial profile esthetics. American journal of orthodontics and dentofacial orthopedics. 2005 Jun 1;127(6):692-9.

15. Skomina Z, Verdenik M, Hren NI. Effect of aging and body characteristics on facial sexual dimorphism in the Caucasian Population. Plos one. 2020 May 14;15(5):e0231983.

16. Mydlova M, Dupej J, Koudelova J, Veleminská J. Sexual dimorphism of facial appearance in ageing human adults: a cross-sectional study. Forensic science international. 2015 Dec 1;257:519-e1.

17. Franco FC, Araujo TM, Vogel CJ, Quintão CC. Brachycephalic, dolichocephalic and mesocephalic: Is it appropriate to describe the face using skull patterns?. Dental press journal of orthodontics. 2013 Jun;18(3):159-63.

18. Bishara SE, Ortho D, Jakobsen JR. Longitudinal changes in three normal facial types. American Journal of Orthodontics. 1985 Dec 1;88(6):466-502.

19. Sassouni V. A classification of skeletal facial types. American journal of orthodontics. 1969 Feb 1;55(2):109-23.

20. Saima Hussain, Vaibhav Joshi, Shobhit Arora, Nada Ali. Facial aesthetics-review International Journal of Current Research. 2015 june 7 (04): 17577-17582.

21. Ahmed HM, Al-Khawaja NF, Nahidh M. Assessment of Palatal Dimensions in a Sample of Iraqi Adults with Different Facial Forms.

22. Hughes GA. Facial types and tooth arrangement. The Journal of prosthetic dentistry. 1951 Jan 1;1(1-2):82-95.

23. Reyneke JP, Ferretti C. Clinical assessment of the face. In Seminars in orthodontics 2012 Sep 1 (Vol. 18, No. 3, pp. 172-186). WB Saunders.

24. Sassouni V. A classification of skeletal facial types. American journal of orthodontics. 1969 Feb 1;55(2):109-23.

25. Vig KW, Fields HW. Facial growth and management of orthodontic problems. Pediatric Clinics of North America. 2000 Oct 1;47(5):1085-123.

26. Sharma P, Arora A, Valiathan A. Age changes of jaws and soft tissue profile. The Scientific World Journal. 2014 Nov;2014.

27. Prahl-Andersen B, Ligthelm-Bakker AS, Wattel E, Nanda R. Adolescent growth changes in soft tissue profile. American Journal of Orthodontics and Dentofacial Orthopedics. 1995 May 1;107(5):476-83.

28. Nanda RS, Meng H, Kapila S, Goorhuis J. Growth changes in the soft tissue facial profile. The Angle Orthodontist. 1990 Sep;60(3):177-90.

29. Subtelny JD. A longitudinal study of soft tissue facial structures and their profile characteristics, defined in relation to underlying skeletal structures. American Journal of Orthodontics. 1959 Jul 1;45(7):481-507.

30. Bloom LA. Perioral profile changes in orthodontic treatment. American Journal of Orthodontics and Dentofacial Orthopedics. 1961 May 1;47(5):371-9.

31. Zylinski CG, Nanda RS, Kapila S. Analysis of soft tissue facial profile in white males. American Journal of Orthodontics and Dentofacial Orthopedics. 1992 Jun 1;101(6):514-8.

32. Blanchette ME, Nanda RS, Currier GF, Ghosh J, Nanda SK. A longitudinal cephalometric study of the soft tissue profile of short-and long face syndromes from 7 to 17 years. American journal of orthodontics and dentofacial orthopedics. 1996 Feb 1;109(2):116-31.

33. Wisth PJ. Changes of the soft tissue profile during growth. The European Journal of Orthodontics. 2007 Apr 1;29(suppl_1):i114-7.

34. Sharma P, Arora A, Valiathan A. Age changes of jaws and soft tissue profile. The Scientific World Journal. 2014 Nov;2014.

35. Prahl-Andersen B, Ligthelm-Bakker AS, Wattel E, Nanda R. Adolescent growth changes in soft tissue profile. American Journal of Orthodontics and Dentofacial Orthopedics. 1995 May 1;107(5):476-83.

36. Garner LD. Soft-tissue changes concurrent with orthodontic tooth movement. American Journal of Orthodontics and Dentofacial Orthopedics. 1974 Oct 1;66(4):367-77.

37. Nanda RS, Ghosh J. Facial soft tissue harmony and growth in orthodontic treatment. In Seminars in orthodontics 1995 Jun 1 (Vol. 1, No. 2, pp. 67-81). WB Saunders.

38. Siqueira DF, da Silva MV, Carvalho PE, do Valle-Corotti KM. The importance of the facial profile in orthodontic diagnosis and treatment planning: a patient report. World journal of orthodontics. 2009 Dec 1;10(4).

39. Mejia-Maidl M, Evans CA. Soft tissue facial considerations andorthodontic treatment. InSeminars in Orthodontics 2000 Mar 1 (Vol. 6, No. 1, pp. 3-20). WB Saunders.

40. Bloom LA. Perioral profile changes in orthodontic treatment. American Journal of Orthodontics and Dentofacial Orthopedics. 1961 May 1;47(5):371-9.

41. Pricillia Priska Sianita. "Facial Profile Changes in Class III Malocclusion through Orthodontic Treatment". EC Dental Science 17.9 (2018): 1582-1591.

42. Kaveh Baharvand Ahmadi, Peter H Buschang, Sawsan Tabbaa. Lip Changes Following NonExtraction Orthodontic Treatment. 4(3). MRD.000587.2019.

43. Mejia-Maidl M, Evans CA. Soft tissue facial considerations andorthodontic treatment. InSeminars in Orthodontics 2000 Mar 1 (Vol. 6, No. 1, pp. 3-20). WB Saunders.

44. Kocadereli I. Changes in soft tissue profile after orthodontic treatment with and without extractions. American Journal of Orthodontics and Dentofacial Orthopedics. 2002 Jul 1;122(1):67-72.

45. Finnöy JP, Wisth PJ, Böe OE. Changes in soft tissue profile during and after orthodontic treatment. The European Journal of Orthodontics. 1987 Jan 1;9(1):68-78.

46. Fitzgerald R, Carqueville J, Yang PT. An approach to structural facial rejuvenation with fillers in women. International journal of women's dermatology. 2019 Feb 1;5(1):52-67.

47. Shome D, Vadera S, Khare S, Ram MS, Ayyar A, Kapoor R, Desai N. Aging and the Indian face: an analytical study of aging in the Asian Indian face. Plastic and Reconstructive Surgery Global Open. 2020 Mar;8(3).

48. Kaur M, Garg RK, Singla S. Analysis of facial soft tissue changes with aging and their effects on facial morphology: A forensic perspective. Egyptian Journal of Forensic Sciences. 2015 Jun 1;5(2):46-56.

49. Chandra HJ, Ravi MS, Sharma SM, Prasad BR. Standards of facial esthetics: an anthropometric study. Journal of maxillofacial and oral surgery. 2012 Dec 1;11(4):384-9.

50. Bashour M. History and current concepts in the analysis of facial attractiveness. Plastic and Reconstructive Surgery. 2006 Sep 1;118(3):741-56.

51. Akter L, Hossain MZ. Angular photogrammetric soft tissue facial profile analysis of Bangladeshi young adults. APOS Trends in Orthodontics. 2017;7(6):279-86.

52. Yılmaz H, Bilgiç F, Akıncı Sözer Ö. Recent photography trends in orthodontics. Turkish J Orthod 2015; 28(3): 113-21

53. Kaur M, Garg RK, Singla S. Analysis of facial soft tissue changes with aging and their effects on facial morphology: A forensic perspective. Egyptian Journal of Forensic Sciences. 2015 Jun 1;5(2):46-56.

54. Soh J, Chew MT, Wong HB. A comparative assessment of the perception of Chinese facial profile esthetics. American journal of orthodontics and dentofacial orthopedics. 2005 Jun 1;127(6):692-9.

55. Yılmaz H, Bilgiç F, Akıncı Sözer Ö. Recent photography trends in orthodontics. Turkish J Orthod 2015; 28(3): 113-21

56. Sharma P, Arora A, Valiathan A. Age changes of jaws and soft tissue profile. The Scientific World Journal. 2014 Nov;2014.

57. Spyropoulos MN, Halazonetis DJ. Significance of the soft tissue profile on facial esthetics. American Journal of Orthodontics and Dentofacial Orthopedics. 2001 May 1;119(5):464-71.

58. Barnett DP. Variations in the soft tissue profile and their relevance to the clinical assessment of skeletal pattern. British journal of orthodontics. 1975 Oct;2(4):235-8.

59. Xuan J, Bing L, Li SF, Ma YN, Kwon TG, Wu XP. Morphological characteristics of soft tissue profile of angle's class II division I malocclusion before and after orthodontic treatment. Int J Morphol. 2018 Mar 1;36(01):26-30.

60. S.M.Asif1 , Y.Muralidhar Reddy2 , C.Sreekanth3 , B.VishnuVardhan Reddy4 Evaluation of Soft Tissue Measurements in Various Skeletal Malocclusions of Kurnool Population- A Cephalometric StudyInternational Journal of Oral Health and Medical Research | ISSN 2395- 7387 | MARCH-APRIL 2016

61. Burke PH, Banks P, Beard LF, Tee JE, Hughes C. Stereophotographic measurement of change in facial soft tissue morphology following surgery. British Journal of Oral Surgery. 1983 Dec 1;21(4):237-45.

62. Sharma P, Arora A, Valiathan A. Age changes of jaws and soft tissue profile. The Scientific World Journal. 2014 Nov;2014.